A BRIEF HISTORY OF
WOODBRIDGE
· NEW JERSEY ·

A BRIEF HISTORY OF
WOODBRIDGE
· NEW JERSEY ·

PHILL PROVANCE

ORIGINAL PHOTOGRAPHS BY MICHAEL PROVANCE

THE
History
PRESS

Published by The History Press
Charleston, SC
www.historypress.net

Front cover, top: An institution in Woodbridge, Amboy Avenue's Reo Diner is also a New Jersey landmark as the first all-night diner in a state known for its all-night diners. *Public domain*; *bottom*: Formally opened in 1927, the fabled Woodbridge Speedway began in 1926 as a dirt track; it was subsequently replaced with wooden and, finally, oiled-dirt tracks. *Woodbridge Township Historic Preservation Society.*
Back cover, top: Before the New Jersey Highway Authority took over the Parkway, taxpayer money completed the eleven-mile stretch around Woodbridge—which is why that section is still toll-free. *Public Library of Massachusetts*; *inset*: Even if World War II wasn't actually the "war to end all wars," Woodbridge's ecstatic homecoming parade, boasting 30,000 attendees, might have been the end-all of parades. *Richard.*

First published 2019

Manufactured in the United States

ISBN 9781467135856

Library of Congress Control Number: 2018966265

Notice: The information in this book is true and complete to the best of our knowledge. It is offered without guarantee on the part of the author or The History Press. The author and The History Press disclaim all liability in connection with the use of this book.

For Pauly and Tom LaGrutta, Deb LaVeglia, Joe Weil and my many other Woodbridge friends, as well as for my family, especially Mike and Ledger

CONTENTS

CONTENTS

FOREWORD

The author of this book has been formally trained in writing. In fact, he is just finishing up his MFA as I write this foreword. I met him a long time ago at a poetry reading that I ran with Edie Eutice (the founder of PoetsWednesday at the Barron Arts Center) and Joe Weil. Back then, it seemed many people were despairing that the discipline in which I was working was a dying field and that there was only one career track left in this area (which is not a very pleasant idea, if that is the way you plan to make your living). I'm talking about an MFA in poetry. But there were a number of us working in the field who believed it an extremely important area for the future. Our optimism and deep belief did not disappoint us. So, a reading series was created where the people of Woodbridge and other local areas could gather together and share their work and their ideas. This is where I first met the author of this book. He was a young writer whose work was interesting, competent and vital, and I am not surprised at all by the high quality of writing contained herein.

When I met Phill Provance, I was a Woodbridge resident myself. My husband and I raised our son on East Grove Avenue. The people of Woodbridge, at least those I've met, have a deep interest in their town. As soon as we moved in, an older couple who lived a few houses away told us stories about our area, that there were once apple orchards and that my house was the mayor's house—which came as a surprise since it was only a very modest Dutch Colonial.

But so it is with Woodbridge that even the most modest things about the town have a certain genius for concealing a wealth of history. And the present volume captures this essence perfectly, for though it is *A Brief History of Woodbridge, New Jersey*, it contains a vast amount of interesting information. Here, there is something for everyone: Provance begins long before the town was settled in 1664, going back in time to tell us about the land itself, about its dinosaur bones and the semi-nomadic Native American peoples who passed through. Then, he goes on to speak of Woodbridge and its original boundaries, which stretched far and wide and encompassed what are now Perth Amboy, Edison, Rahway and more. This was a surprise for me, for I myself lived in Sewaren briefly, and once, while walking along the water, I met an older fellow who told me about how, from where we stood, his father used to catch the "showboats" (floating theaters) that periodically came and offered entertainment for an affordable price.

What's more, this book tells of James Parker, who was born in Woodbridge and apprenticed with Benjamin Franklin. And we discover the part Woodbridge played in the early antislavery movement. Plus, if you're interested in the wars that shaped our nation, Provance writes beautifully of Woodbridge and the Revolution, the War of 1812, the Civil War and World Wars I and II. And, yes, George Washington did sleep here: he spent a night at the Cross Keys Tavern, which was then located on the northwest corner of Amboy Avenue and Main Street in a building that, as Provance notes, still stands today.

But, most of all, there's magic here. I believe with this book Provance has done the difficult work of capturing our imaginations while also teaching us the history of a town. And it struck me that, from beginning to end, he has included, amid the facts and dates, names and words, a love and devotion to the township of Woodbridge and a dedication to history, beginnings and home.

Deborah LaVeglia
Director, Barron Arts Center

ACKNOWLEDGEMENTS

For any author, the first book in any genre, no matter the scope, is always daunting. But in the case of *A Brief History of Woodbridge, New Jersey*, it was made especially so due to my own boneheaded decision to tackle my first full-length work of nonfiction at the same time as I was completing my MFA. Of course, all the while I was teaching private writing classes and finishing my first full-length poetry collection, plus—most importantly—coparenting the best person ever to come into my life, my son, Ledger. Therefore, special thanks are due to a long list of friends and family who put up with my two-year attempt to cram it all in at once, but especially to Ledger's mother, Allison Eir Jenks, who took on more than her fair share of the responsibility to give me the time I needed, and to Ledger himself, who (though I tried to keep it to a minimum) missed out on at least a couple romps in the park because Daddy needed to work. For your patience, I am grateful to you both, and I promise, Little Bear, now that this little book of mine is done, we'll be making up for lost time.

Moreover, heartfelt thanks are due to my brother Mike, who sacrificed his morning one Saturday to train his talents on capturing many of the photographs of modern Woodbridge included in this book; to my stepfather, J.C., who encouraged me to pitch the present work to Stevie Edwards at The History Press; to my mother, Mary, and father, David, for their continuous encouragement over three decades—since, indeed, my little hands set their first squiggly "o" down on paper; to my many friends in Woodbridge, including Paul and Tom LaGrutta, whose encouragement to "get a real job" the summer I waited tables for them fifteen years ago set me on my current path and inspired the present work; to Professor Joe Weil of SUNY Binghamton and Woodbridge Barron Arts Center director Deborah LaVeglia, both of whom are amazing poets and both of whom have not only continued to encourage my writing over the years but were originally responsible for prodding me to read at my first open mic; to Dr. Jerry Brown of Sewaren for opening his home and making his vast personal collection of Woodbridge-related research materials available to me as this project was getting underway; and to Woodbridge Public Library archivist and Woodbridge Township Historic Preservation Commission commissioner Wendi Rottweiler, who first sparked my interest in Woodbridge's history by taking me on as her assistant when I worked as a clerk at the Woodbridge Public Library.

Finally, thanks are due to History Press editors Amanda Irle and Adam Ferrell for their patience and understanding in moving back my deadline several times and giving me the extra words to cover it all, to Sara Miller for lending her highly talented editorial eye to knocking this project into shape, and to Stevie Edwards for first approaching me about working with The History Press, as well as to the entire THP team and the many mentors and educators who have gone above and beyond in encouraging me and helping me improve my writing, including Drs. Larry Grimes and Walt Turner and professor Anthony Mitch, formerly of Bethany College; Dr. Zachary Schomburg; professor Mark Lamoureux of Housatonic Community College; professor Marvin Bell of Pacific University; Dr. Allison Eir Jenks; and, especially, Drs. Mark Defoe and Devon McNamara and professors Jessie van Eerden, Richard Schmitt, Doug Van Gundy, Mary Carroll-Hackett, Diane Gilliam, Katie Fallon, Karen McElmurray, Jacinda Townsend and Kim Dana Kupperman of West Virginia Wesleyan's MFA program, who have not only taught me to string words together better but have shown me how to make any book worth reading no matter its scope and audience.

INTRODUCTION

Returning to New Jersey to visit family each summer, I make a point of visiting Woodbridge just to walk. Where I go depends on my mood, the time of day and the weather. But mostly I follow Rahway Avenue through the tree-lined serenity of the old city greens, then either head on to the bustle of Main Street—where I'll grab a pick-me-up in the cool shelter of J.J. Bitting's—or stroll past the well-kept lawns and sunny facades of Freeman Street's Cape Cods and colonials. Thus wandering the town whistling, I like to pretend I'm Andy Griffith, meandering for several hours through my old neighborhood before doubling back for a steak dinner and a flight of cocktails with longtime friend Paul LaGrutta and his staff at Mulberry Street Restaurant.

Of course, the reason for my fascination with the town after so many years away is straightforward as anyone's: it's hard to live in Woodbridge for any amount of time without leaving behind a piece of yourself. As for me, I can say without much qualification that many of the most important moments of my early adulthood happened in Woodbridge, from the beginnings of my writing career to the first time I ever got behind the wheel of a car—with my terrified driving instructor clutching the dash beside me. So, in a very real sense, Woodbridge made me the freewheeling literary man I am today and, when The History Press asked me to pitch a nonfiction book, I could think of no other project I wanted to work on more than giving back to the town with an end-all summation of its fascinating 350-year history.

Left: As if I need any more encouragement, the first landmark I always pass heading into Woodbridge is the huge "EAT" sign outside Iselin's Jose Tejas. *Ted Kerwin.*

Right: My last excuse for visiting Woodbridge? I'm still a member of the Woodbridge Elks (Lodge No. 2116), so, naturally, I came for Bike Night in May 2017. *Michael Provance.*

And yet, truth be told, what I had in mind—and what I hope you now hold in your hands—was no small order. You see, my aim in writing *A Brief History of Woodbridge, New Jersey*, was to create something altogether different: a brief small-town history, yes, but one that reads like any fine work of creative nonfiction. I figured if Thornton Wilder's historical novel *The Bridge of San Luis Rey* could be about a little-known bridge in a little-known corner of the world, why couldn't I write a lovable book about a town as steeped in history as Woodbridge? Granted, I'm no Thornton Wilder, but the whole concept still doesn't seem implausible. Then again, dear reader, the ultimate judgment of how wide or narrow of the proverbial mark I've struck always and only rests with you.

Moreover, nothing you're about to read would have been possible without the hard work of Woodbridge's many previous historians, including Joseph Dally, Virginia Troeger, Robert McEwen and Gordon Bond, as well as the dozens of newspaper and magazine journalists whose articles filled in the gaps for me. If the serious local historian is seeking source material, I can do no better than refer her to these luminaries, qualifying that there is so

Erected in the 1990s, Woodbridge Township's modern municipal building overlooks
the three-way intersection where Berry Street, Rahway Avenue and Main Street meet.
Michael Provance.

much more to Woodbridge history contained in their books than I could
have possibly included in my own brief, *popular* history of the town.

Thus, *A Brief History of Woodbridge, New Jersey*, is intended to inform, yes,
but even more importantly, I hope it conveys the sense of kinetic excitement
that has buzzed about Woodbridge since its first European residents began
clearing the wilderness where we now see highways, homes and office
buildings. Then, with any luck, perhaps this excitement will drive you to the
many sources listed in the bibliography section at the back of this book. But
even if that doesn't happen, at the very least, I hope you'll be as entranced
as I've been by the many tragic, hilarious and just plain weird incidents
that have made Woodbridge what it is today. After all, often the very heady
feeling we dream of finding far afield is available to us in spades just outside
our front doors. With Woodbridge, I've discovered, this is certainly true, and
I hope that with my own small contribution to the town's history, I will prove
it to you as well.

Phill Provance
February 5, 2018

CHAPTER I

SO, WHERE'S THE WOODEN BRIDGE?

Prehistory to the Township Charter

For anyone new to Woodbridge, the first question that usually comes to mind is, "So, where's the wooden bridge?" As for that, the truth is that, sure, Woodbridge has had plenty of bridges made of wood, but *the* wooden bridge never existed—or if it did, it was in England. Woodbridge, it must be remembered, got its name in the same manner as most English settlements in colonial America—from the name of the town its founders had left. There is indeed a Woodbridge in the United Kingdom in Suffolk, East Anglia, and it's a pleasant little spot, much like its namesake, located about a two-hour drive northeast of London. An alternative explanation has it that perhaps the town was named for Reverend John Woodbridge IV, a famed Nonconformist minister preaching in seventeenth-century New England around the time that the town's very first English founders wove their way along the Atlantic coastline from the Massachusetts, Connecticut, Rhode Island and New York colonies into what would become New Jersey. But this latter hypothesis is mostly conjecture, as local historians Virginia Troeger and Robert McEwen point out; simply put, it doesn't hold up when we consider the dozens of other towns with the same name throughout the United States, Canada and Australia. Truth be told, since naming your new hometown after your old haunt was the order of the day in the American colonies, it is probably only Reverend Woodbridge's relation to the Parkers of New England and his promotion of America's first poet, Anne Bradstreet (he was her brother-in-law and integral to the publication of her work), that has kept this rumor alive.

In any event, though, *how* Woodbridge got its name is a minor detail beside the question of *where* its first residents came from. When New Jersey's first English governor, Philip Carteret, first alighted on Newark Bay (as yet still "Achter Kol") from the S.S. *Philip* in his dainty black wig and neatly ribboned straights in August 1665, European settlement of the area was already well underway. So, his party of thirty men and women and the ragtag band of Dutch and English colonists who greeted them were likely too shocked at seeing each other to worry about place names. Up to that point, you see, the colonists had been under the impression that they were in New York, while Governor Carteret, taking his commission from his cousin and colonial proprietor Sir George Carteret, had thought he was landing in the colony of New Jersey.

As we'll see, both groups ultimately found that their new home would continue to defy their expectations. But, before we get into all that, let's first digress a bit to learn what European expansion into the Woodbridge area during what historians call "the Columbian Exchange" would eventually end. After all, to say there were people in Woodbridge before Governor Carteret first landed is utter understatement. In addition to the unexpected European colonists already in New Jersey when Governor Carteret arrived, there were also the region's native Lenape inhabitants, as well as numerous species of trees and flowers, animals, birds and fish—many of which no longer exist in the Woodbridge area, having been replaced by European species brought by English and Dutch colonists looking to reproduce their old ways of life.

The Time Before Landing: Prehistoric Woodbridge and the Lenni-Lenape

Before 1609, as town historian Joseph Dally relates in his 1873 history, *Woodbridge and Vicinity*, the land Woodbridge now occupies was covered in wild cherry, sumac, sassafras and flax and populated by deer, wolves, otter, red and gray foxes, raccoons, squirrels, mink, rabbits, beavers, pheasants, plovers, wild ducks and wild pigeons so plentiful that their flocks reportedly darkened the sky. What's more, the Arthur Kill, located off the coast of modern Sewaren, was rife with perch, eels, oysters, clams and other tasty sea critters that regularly appeared on Lenape and, later, colonial dinner plates.

This page: Before Public Service and Gas, Hess Oil and Shell Oil dominated Sewaren, the Arthur Kill was home to hordes of perch, eels, oysters and clams. *Top, EPA; bottom, National Archives.*

A Brief History of Woodbridge, New Jersey

As for the land's topography, as Virginia Troeger and Robert J. McEwen describe in their 2002 history, *Woodbridge: New Jersey's Oldest Township*, sediments carried down the Hudson and Delaware Rivers by glacial melt in the late Lower Cretaceous Age formed the site where Woodbridge now sits—what geologists call the Piedmont Plateau. Because of this estuarial origin, the land between the Arthur Kill and Raritan rivers is rich in loamy soils ideal for agriculture. In fact, as several now-lost fossilized footprints first found by Roy E. Anderson in the Hampton Cutter clay banks off Amboy Avenue in January and March 1930 once attested, Woodbridge has always been a fertile spot. As for the footprints themselves (of a three-toed dinosaur later identified by the American Museum of Natural History's Dr. Barnum Brown as a carnivore), they are notably the only dinosaur footprints from the Cretaceous period that anyone has found east of the Mississippi River.

And so, Woodbridge was always prime real estate, even before the concept of "real estate" existed. At least, that's how humanity found it around ten thousand years ago, when the Algonquin ancestors of Woodbridge's first human inhabitants, the Lenni-Lenape, or "original people," moved eastward into the region and spread up and down the Atlantic coastline. Though some modern Lenape live in Minisink in Sussex County, New Jersey, little reliable information about their pre-Columbian culture survives because they were one of the first groups to interact with European settlers. Since they didn't have a written language prior to the introduction of Dutch and English, what we know was frequently recorded by European observers or adulterated by attempts among seventeenth-, eighteenth- and nineteenth-century Lenape to assimilate by justifying their culture to a Eurocentric audience.

What is certain, though, is that two major language groups of Lenape lived in or around Woodbridge at the time of European contact: the Munsee (north of the Raritan) and the Northern Unami, or "river people" (south of the Raritan). These two related groups thought of themselves as distinct, though they all fell under the aegis of the Nanticoke peoples, who lived in New York, eastern Pennsylvania, Maryland, Delaware and New Jersey. What's more, the Lenape were socially divided into tribes including the Wolf, Turtle and Turkey tribes, which were, in turn, divided into twelve clans further subdivided into individual villages; according to modern Lenape, men and women were expected to seek partners from one of the two other tribes, a practice presumably meant to avoid thinning the gene pool.

As for which specific groups of Lenape resided in the Woodbridge area, a Dutch map from 1656 notes the area is populated by "Sanhicans," meaning "stone tools." But this might have been the result of a miscommunication.

This twentieth-century photo shows one of Woodbridge's clay pits, where the only Cretaceous-period dinosaur footprints east of the Mississippi were found in 1930. *EPA.*

Other histories record that the Lenape village groups in the Woodbridge area included the Raritans, or "Raritons" (also known as the "Naraticongs") and Navesinks (or Nevesinks), who spoke the Munsee dialect. Further, other groups recorded as moving through the Woodbridge area include the Pomptons, an Algonquin tribe that spoke the Unami dialect, and the Mantas (possibly a clan of the Lenape Wolf Tribe).

But nailing down exactly how many Lenape groups existed in the area prior to the Columbian Exchange is nearly impossible due to the sheer size of the Lenape population and their cultural practices. Some contemporary scholars, for instance, have estimated that ten to twelve thousand Lenape lived in the Woodbridge area in the seventeenth century, while others have said fifteen thousand lived in eighty settlements in or around what is now New York City. Another issue with providing an accurate headcount, moreover, is that no village stayed in the same spot year-round. You see, the Lenape were matrilineal, meaning that an individual's social identity passed through his or her mother's side, and semiagrarian, meaning they grew the "three sisters"—winter squash, maize (or corn) and climbing beans. They also hunted for their meat and caught fish and shellfish. So, while they used slash-and-burn techniques to clear land for their crops, seeding their fields with nutrients from controlled fires, they would also move between locales depending on the season and the movements of game animals, birds and fish. Thus, though the Lenape would return to their villages each winter, they were often enough elsewhere, and many others passed through the area known to the Lenape as *Ambo*, or "the Point," creating a situation that was so fluid that the area's Munsee Lenape had to fortify their villages by surrounding them with palisades to ward against attacks from marauding Mohawks.

Apparently, these raids did not pass the boundary of the Raritan River, for no evidence exists that the Unami and Unalactigo villages were fortified. But, on the whole, little other reliable information of the original Lenape lifestyle survives, and what information is now available is often contradictory. To some, for instance, the "Minisink" was a valley in northwestern New Jersey where a group of Munsee Lenape lived, while to others, as noted by Troeger and McEwen, it was a major trail extending from the mouths of the Navesink and Shrewsburys Rivers through what would become Woodbridge. The likely culprit for this confusion is the language barrier between Europeans and the Lenape. So, reconstructing the pre-Columbian Lenape world, while not entirely impossible, is a fraught proposition for any historian.

A bit of history to reflect on next time you're plowing through a nor'easter: today's Parkway and Turnpike originated from Lenape footpaths. *Public domain.*

What is certain is that, though their population would drop to just a few hundred individuals by the American Revolution due to the combined effects of European diseases, violence and displacement, these earliest Woodbridge inhabitants left an indelible mark on the town. Not only did they coin dozens of words that still survive as place names—including Amboy, Cheesequake, Hoboken, Hopatcong, Netcong, Matawan, Manasquan, Metuchen, Passaic, Papiack, Peapack, Rahway and Watchung, as well as Rarachons or Wawitan, meaning "forked river," from which the Dutch coined today's "Raritan"—they also effectively built the area's first highways in the form of their many paths. The Minisink Trail, for instance, would eventually become a roadway for European settlers, as would the Lenape's Allamatunk Trail, which skirted the town along its path from the Delaware Water Gap to New Brunswick. Thus, in some sense, the pre-Columbian Lenape were also the original architects of the highway interchange in Woodbridge that so many New Jersey inhabitants regularly drive on today.

Braving the New World: European Settlement in Woodbridge

The Europeans' first forays into the territory known as the Lenapehoking came in 1609, when English explorer Henry Hudson sailed up the river that now bears his name (then known as the "North River") in his ship, the *Half Moon*. By then, Europeans had long been in the habit of mislabeling the New World peoples they encountered as "Indians"—even after it had become apparent that the lands they'd "discovered" in the fifteenth and sixteenth centuries weren't part of Asia—and of claiming those peoples' lands for themselves. So, having navigated the Delaware and Hudson Rivers, the New Jersey coastline and the Connecticut River, Hudson claimed it all for his Dutch patrons, and thus was born the colony of Nieuw Nederland.

The first Dutch settlement in the area began in 1621 with the organization of the Dutch West India Company and the settlement of Governor's Island in 1624. Subsequently, then, Fort Amsterdam was built in 1625, and its commander, General Peter Minuit, purchased Manhattan Island in 1626 from its Lenape inhabitants for 60 guilders. Soon thereafter, the site of Minuit's purchase became the small trading post Nieuw Amsterdam, which sat amid the militarily and economically choice confluence of the Hudson, Achter Kol and Raritan Rivers on the Atlantic seacoast. And, because the region was flush with the millions of beavers needed to make the broad-brimmed, beaver-skin hats fashionable among Dutch men at the time, this trading outpost quickly grew into the thriving commercial center now known as New York City.

And yet, it still remained to be seen whether New Amsterdam would pass into English hands, since a 1655 Swedish attempt to wrest it from the Dutch was quickly repelled by Nieuw Nederland's strongman governor, Peter Stuyvesant. The change of hands, however, could not come soon enough for the English, since their Massachusetts and Virginia colonies were effectively cut off from each other and strategically compromised by the Dutch settlement. So, in 1665, the English sent Colonel Richard Nicolls with a much larger invading force than the Swedes had mustered, and this was apparently a large enough inducement to convince Stuyvesant to give up the proverbial ghost.

Thus, having acquired the territory from Stuyvesant without bloodshed, Nicolls quickly began issuing land grants to the many disaffected Puritans flooding in from New England. However, in terms of who "owned" the land at this point, there was still a bit of a hang-up: King Charles II had already granted the portion of land that would become New Jersey to his brother James, Duke of York and Albany, in 1664—before it had been won from the Dutch; indeed, it was this grant that had precipitated the launch of Nicolls's invasion force of four ships, for James had, naturally, wanted to ensure his right to govern a colony he already supposedly owned. Then, to make matters worse, neither Nicolls nor the Duke of York were the greatest communicators. For instance, Nicolls was completely unaware that on June 24, 1664, while he was still at sea, the duke had given the land between the Hudson and Delaware Rivers to court favorites Sir George Carteret and John, Lord Berkeley, naming the deeded territory "Nova Caesarea or New Jersey." Nor were Carteret and Berkeley aware that Nicolls had OK'd a petition from Jamaica, Long Island, land speculators John Bailey, Daniel Denton and Luke Watson to purchase five hundred thousand acres of what was to be New Jersey from Staten Island Lenape chief Mattano.

Hence, as noted above, when Sir George's cousin Philip Carteret alighted from his ship to take up his governorship, there were already several dozen settlers who felt they had legal rights to the land on which Woodbridge, "Elizabethtown" (now Elizabeth), Piscataway, Middletown and Shrewsbury now exist. In fact, Elizabeth, the colony's first capital, already consisted of four wooden houses that Bailey, Denton and Watson had built to take legal possession from the Lenape, who had delivered

New Jersey separated from New York in 1664, when Sir George Carteret (*above*) and John, Lord Berkeley, acquired the territory from the Duke of York. *Public domain.*

the deed of conveyance to the Long Islanders on December 1, 1664. Worse still, from Carteret's perspective, those who had purchased tracts from Bailey, Denton and Watson were predominantly religious outcasts and uppity commoners from New England who had come for Nicolls's promises of moderate religious tolerance, self-taxation, a five-year tax holiday, universal suffrage for all men who weren't slaves or hired laborers and opportunities to own land and hold public office. The stage was set for a showdown between the colonies of New York and New Jersey in an imbroglio that wouldn't fully work itself out for nearly a century.

In the meantime, though, Governor Carteret had to get settled in, and his first order of business was to name the settlement started by Bailey, Denton and Watson "Elizabeth Towne"—either after the wife of his patron and cousin, Sir George, or after his own wife. Then, he and his entourage began building their own homes in Elizabeth, and gathering from the "Elizabethtown Associates"—as Bailey, Denton and Watson were calling themselves—that some misunderstanding was afoot, he sent word across Newark Bay to Governor Richard Nicolls that the rightful owners had put him in charge.

In response, Nicolls complained to the Duke of York, but as Nicolls was something of a hired hand himself, these messages went ignored. The problem with the "Nicolls claims," the respective proprietors of New York and New Jersey assumed, would iron itself out after the military governor was replaced. And so, in 1668, after Governor Nicolls had served a term of just four years, the duke filled New York's gubernatorial seat with Sir Edmond Andros and hoped that would be the end of the matter. Meanwhile, Governor Carteret set to work attempting to undo Nicolls's promises that were most obnoxious to the Lords Proprietors (Lord Berkeley and Sir George), namely the notion of self-taxation. You see, the New Jersey colony was supposed to pay them dividends; the colony, from their perspective, was a corporation, and how else could it yield a return on investment if the colonists weren't paying for the privilege of living there? Indeed, Governor Carteret was more a CEO than a governing official, so his next order of business was to offer the colonists a new—if somewhat less desirable—deal, *The Concessions and Agreements of the Lords Proprietors of the Province of New Caesarea or New Jersey*. In it, he retained many of Nicolls's promises of self-governance and religious tolerance but required property owners (known as freeholders) to pay an annual tax (or quitrent) to the proprietors starting in 1670.

Suffice it to say, Carteret's quitrents weren't what those who had purchased their land directly from the Lenape (especially in Elizabeth and Piscataway) had bargained for; they had expected to make a jump in class, to become land-owning gentry by settling in New Jersey. What they ended up with, meanwhile, was pretty much the same feudal tithing system they'd left behind in England. So began what New Jersey historians now term the antiproprietary movement and land wars, which would eventually spell the end of Carteret's tenure as governor. Nor would matters get any less complicated as time went on, for just two years later, another group of colonists began entering the territory across the ten-mile stretch of salt marsh south of Elizabeth, these folks having totally ducked the Nicolls-Carteret confusion by purchasing legitimate land patents from Massachusetts Puritan speculators Daniel Pierce and Associates. The fact was, it would seem, New Jersey was going to become a land of haves (including the proprietors and those with favored grants) and have-nots (those with Nicholls' grants), and there was little by way of law enforcement to keep the two groups from fighting.

The Pierce and Associates settlers were, of course, the first freeholders of what would become Woodbridge, and by surveying the land they purchased on December 3, 1667, they signaled their intention to stay. Among them, in addition to Daniel Pierce, were John Bishop, John Crandel, Benjamin Cromwell, Samuel Dennis, Peter Dessigny, William Elston, John French, Samuel Hale, Adam Hude, John Ilsly, Henry Jaquis, George Lockhart, Hugh March, John Mootry, Benjamin Parker, Elisha Parker, John Robeson, John Robinson, John Smith, John Smith the Scotchman, John Taylor and John Watkins. But this is merely the original roll of freeholders, or landowners, who would pay no other fee for their land than the annual quitrent to the Lords Proprietors. According to Troeger and McEwen, 120 additional persons came with the first setters as slaves, and there is no surviving record listing the landless workers (called freemen) and indentured servants who also came. Throughout the early part of 1667, several additional freeholders would join these men and their families, and in mid-November 1667, Woodbridge reached its first milestone with the birth of Mary Compton, daughter of Mary and William Compton and the first child born of European settlers in the area; on June 1, 1669, it reached its second when King Charles II granted it a township charter.

SEEK AND YE SHALL FIND: WOODBRIDGE'S SEARCH FOR A MINISTER

The two hundred acres of upland and meadows set aside in Woodbridge's 1669 charter for the town minister are (at least partially) the very same land on which today's First Presbyterian and Trinity Episcopal Churches now sit. However, despite these two churches' being two of the town's oldest institutions and most interesting architectural landmarks, the land they now occupy originally held nothing more than the town's graveyard and meetinghouse, which served as a venue for both local government meetings and for nondenominational Christian services. Indeed, the site on which the meetinghouse stood was not specifically reserved for Presbyterian services until the eighteenth century, after the Presbyterian church of Woodbridge secured its charter in 1756.

Until that charter, the history of religion in Woodbridge remained a series of fiascos. And, not for nothing, this had more to do with sectarian infighting, kooky ministers and plain happenstance than it did with the town fathers. In fact, they, having originally hailed from Massachusetts, were all deeply religious men who wanted the Christian gospel preached in their town so much that they didn't particularly care whose version of it got preached. Thus, starting in 1669, immediately following King Charles II's ratification of the town's charter, they sent freeholders George Little and Samuel Moore to Newark to offer the post to one "Mr. Pierson the Younger," son of Newark's Puritan minister.

The problem was, however, that no sooner had Little and Moore arrived in Newark than they learned that Reverend Pierson had fallen ill, and his son had taken up his duties. Thus, the town was forced to settle instead

Minuscule compared with today's municipal building, the original Woodbridge meetinghouse was built in 1682 where Rahway Avenue's Old White Church now stands. *Michael Provance.*

for the yearlong tenure of a local missionary named Treat (or "Teat"), who would be followed by two other more or less short-term ministers, Reverend Benjamin Solsbury (1674) and Reverend John Allen (1680–92). Of these ministers, Allen stayed the longest, but even he didn't seem keen on taking a permanent post in a town that, up to his arrival, had only had nine total months of preaching in its first decade. Maybe, the town worthies aside, Woodbridge's average settler was too raucous a fellow to attend services on Sundays. Whatever the reason for the town's dearth of men of the cloth in the hyper-religious colonies, Woodbridge's records don't note it.

All of this was to change when luck or providence (however you want to figure it) carried Presbyterianism to Amboy Harbor (now Perth Amboy) in 1695. That year, a group of wind-tossed Presbyterian political refugees arrived on the *Henry & Francis* after their deportation from Scotland for refusing to recognize King James II as head of the Presbyterian Kirk (or Church) of Scotland. Thus, according to Robert Wodrow's *A History of the Sufferings of the Church of Scotland from the Restoration to the Revolution*, the whole existence of the First Presbyterian Church of Woodbridge can be chalked up to the ill-fated 1685 invasion of lowland Scotland by the Covenanters, hardline Scottish Presbyterians, under Archibald Campbell, 9th Earl of Argyll.

The long and short of the backstory is that the Covenanters refused to take an oath of allegiance to King James (both James II of England and James VII of Scotland) because, while the oath allowed them to swear allegiance to the Presbyterian church, it also required they acknowledge James, a Catholic, as head of the Kirk. They objected to this because it would, in their view, place the Pope in charge—a deal-breaker for anyone who wanted the Kirk ruled by the Presbyters, or church elders. Following the collapse of Argyll's Rising, then, several of his followers who'd been captured were held at Dunnottar Castle, from whence they were marched on to Leith, where a majority still refused to swear the above-mentioned oath. As a result, they were banished to the American colonies, with those who could not pay their own passage automatically given over as indentured servants to George Scot, Laird of Pitlochie, a Covenanter nobleman who had published extensive philosophizing on American colonization and, consequently, received five hundred acres from the East Jersey government to put his "money where his mouth was." So, a group consisting of Scot, his family and a boatload of former Argyll supporters who both could and could not pay their own passage set sail for what was then East Jersey on the *Henry & Francis* on September 5, 1685, with one Richard Hutton as their shipmaster.

Replacing the town's original meetinghouse in 1803, Woodbridge's Old White Church got its start in 1695, when storm-tossed Scottish Covenanters arrived in Perth Amboy. *Michael Provance.*

To raise funds for the voyage, Scot had offered to release the indentures of any who paid him five pounds sterling prior to setting sail. But, perhaps realizing the illegality of their situation, few of the exiles took him up on the bargain. Then, Pitlochie and his wife, along with many other passengers, died of a fever that flared up among those who had previously been held at Dunnottar. According to Wodrow's description of events, the sickness was due to the awful treatment the Dunnottar prisoners had experienced and the fact that the food procured for the journey had begun to rot even before they'd left Britain. Still, whatever the cause, eventually, everyone on the ship got sick, and while there are varying accounts of how many actually died (some say thirty-one, others as many as seventy), by the time the ship reached Perth Amboy that December, a sizable number of bodies had been thrown overboard during the voyage—supposedly at a rate of three or four bodies a day!

What's more, the survivors had to contend with an unsympathetic shipmaster who had apparently forbidden those who hadn't paid their own passage from holding religious services below deck; according to Wodrow, Hutton would have his crew throw planks of wood at the passengers if they even attempted to pray. And this was the least of his abuses: the captain also tried to convince Pitlochie's son-in-law and heir, one Mr. Johnston, to let him turn the ship toward Virginia or Jamaica, where they could sell the indentured servants at a premium! But, though Johnston was apparently amenable to the proposal, the ship, which was already in such a state of disrepair that it had sprung two leaks during the trip, was caught in a storm and forced to anchor at Perth Amboy.

It was at this point, then, that Woodbridge's freeholders, having learned of the Covenanters' plight, invited the whole kit and caboodle to settle in their town. However, Johnston still had a trick up his sleeve before Woodbridge's first Presbyterians could accept the town's offer: he forced the survivors to sign four-year indentures before he'd let them disembark.

And so it was that Woodbridge hosted these poor, long-suffering refugees through the winter, likely at the town's expense. Then, the following spring, the freeholders also came to the aid of their new neighbors when Johnston attempted to force the issue of his indentures. A court case ensued, with the eventual outcome that, since the Covenanters had been forced into a voyage they couldn't refuse and hadn't received any payment besides, holding them to indenture was inconsistent with East Jersey law. Well, we might imagine that Johnston's head just about exploded at this, and he immediately appealed to his connections among the colony's proprietors.

Built in 1861 after the Episcopalians' first church burned down, today's Trinity Episcopal Church building was inspired by a sermon George Keith delivered in 1702. *Michael Provance.*

Ultimately, though, if Johnston did pull any strings, it resulted in very little. The only vindication he possibly received was the brief jailing on spurious charges of freeholder Samuel Dennis, who, as president of the Middlesex County Court from 1686 to 1687, likely presided over the hearing that set the Woodbridge Covenanters free. Otherwise, the town experienced no other trouble over the matter. Indeed, on the whole, its kindness paid off,

Now called the "Aaron Dunn House" for its Revolutionary resident, 12 Freeman Street was originally the Town House built by Reverend Riddell in the 1690s. *Michael Provance.*

since among the refugees were Adam Hude—who would eventually serve as a town justice, a judge for the Middlesex Court of Common Pleas and a representative to the colonial General Assembly—and Reverend Archibald Riddell, who would end up so popular in Woodbridge that the town would name "Bald Hill" for him, possibly as much for the nickname "Bald" or "Baldy" (from "Archibald") as for his hairless pate.

RIDDELL WOULD EVENTUALLY RETURN to Britain after the Glorious Revolution. But, by then, Woodbridge was pretty much sold on Presbyterianism, so its congregation not only continued in the center of town—where it would eventually build the much-loved "Old White Church"—but became more or less Woodbridge's primary sect up to the mid-1700s. Nor does the history of the Woodbridge Presbyterians really settle down following the tumultuous passage of the Covenanters. For, around the same time that the town's first settlers were passing away, the departure of Reverend Samuel Shepherd would spark a quarter-century of sectarian infighting in the town. All this started with a job offer Woodbridge extended to Shepherd in 1701, which included a yearly salary of sixty pounds sterling in foodstuffs, use of the Town House (built by Riddell near the greens) and a land grant of thirty acres in return for him becoming the town's permanent minister. According to Joseph Dally, this was practically the town bending over backward to keep Shepherd. But to Alice Shepherd, the reverend's wife, it was a pittance. Then, Quaker apostate George Keith came to Woodbridge as a missionary for the Episcopalian Society of the Gospel in Foreign Parts: on his way out the door, on December 30, 1702, Reverend Shepherd allowed Keith to preach a sermon on I Timothy 3:16 in the meetinghouse, and, suddenly, there was a large number of Episcopalians in Woodbridge.

Of course, to be sure, Keith was no favorite among Woodbridge's Quakers at that point (as we'll discuss in a later chapter), and letting him preach was a radical act on Shepherd's part. After all, as mentioned later in this chapter, the Salem witch trials had just occurred during the previous decade, and this was just twenty years since the town's original Presbyterians had been set adrift from Scotland on a death ship for their religious intransigence. So, suffice it to say, despite the relative religious liberty afforded by the colony's charter, tolerance wasn't exactly the rule of the day. Nor, does it seem, was tolerance a virtue Reverend Shepherd shared with his successor, Reverend Nathaniel Wade, who replaced Shepherd as Woodbridge's Presbyterian minister in 1707 and was ordained in 1708. Wade, you see, was of the firebrand variety of New England ministers and an ally of that infamous orchestrator of the Salem witch trials himself, Cotton Mather.

Apparently, enough Woodbridge residents were disgusted by Wade's fire-and-brimstone brand of Christianity that they abandoned the town's Presbyterian services upon his ordination. Instead, beginning in 1707, they started meeting with itinerant Episcopalian missionary John Brook in Piscataway, Rahway and Amboy and, after Brook was lost at sea, with Reverend Edward Vaughn in Elizabeth in 1709. Moreover, Wade alienated even more townsfolk when he submitted the Woodbridge Presbyterian congregation to the rule of the Philadelphia Presbytery in 1710, effectively ending the church's independent status. This led to an even greater defection so that, soon, plenty of Woodbridge residents were attending Episcopalian services just next door to the meetinghouse at Benjamin Dunham's home. By 1711, then, Vaughn needed assistance. He temporarily received it from Perth Amboy's new rector, Reverend Thomas Halliday, but the state of

FIRST PRESBYTERIAN CHURCH, WOODBRIDGE, N. J.

Above: A late–nineteenth century postcard of the Old White Church with a Victorian facade as it appeared after renovations were made in 1875 to mark the first United States centennial. *Public domain.*

Left: The Kirk Green, site of the First Presbyterian Church's cemetery, became something of a battleground when firebrand Reverend Nathaniel Wade butted heads with Woodbridge's Episcopalians. *Michael Provance.*

35

affairs was apparently more than even two ministers could handle, causing Halliday to write to the Society of the Gospel in Foreign Parts complaining that the Woodbridge Episcopalians' meeting place had "no surplice, no bible, no common Table," and was no more than "an old broken house insufficient to keep us from the injuries of the weather."

As a result, the respective situations for both congregations were becoming so dire by the following year that the Episcopalians began demanding their own church even as the Presbyterians voted to eject Reverend Wade, temporarily replacing him with a Reverend Gillespie from the Philadelphia Presbytery. The Woodbridge Episcopalians applied to Governor Robert Hunter for a license to build, while Reverend Wade scurried up to Boston to tattle to Cotton Mather. The outcome of the application was that Governor Hunter—perhaps aware of the uproar Wade had caused and wishing to stem further strife between the two denominations—granted the Episcopalians a license for the lot originally set aside for the town church in "Blazing Star" (today's Carteret) and even subscribed five pounds sterling of his own money to the new church's construction. The governor's largess notwithstanding, however, Woodbridge's Episcopalians didn't take the hint and continued holding their services on the Kirk Green, alternating between the Dunham House and (in good weather) the half-finished church that, in 1712, they began constructing (but never fully completed) on a lot the town voted to give them—thus explaining how the Dunham House still serves as Trinity Episcopal Church's rectory today.

Meanwhile, Reverend Wade returned with one of Mather's agents, the mysterious "Mr. Wiswall," who seems to have been sent by the insidious Mather as both muscle to back up Wade's claim to the Presbyterian pulpit and, barring that, to perhaps act as a spy. Forthwith, Wade and Gillespie had it out, and Gillespie tucked tail, leaving the pulpit again in Wade's hands. The fact that Wiswall returned to New England immediately after Gillespie's ouster seems shady in the extreme, and we can only imagine what "inducements" he and Wade presented to Gillespie to precipitate the interim minister's speedy departure. But, as this was apparently a cloak-and-dagger affair orchestrated by Mather, no record of what transpired comes down to us.

At any rate, though, come 1714, Wade had again foisted himself upon the people of Woodbridge, while the nearby Episcopalians' aspirations for their own church were stymied by the death of their greatest early benefactor, consummate Wade-hater (and son of the town's original miller) Benjamin Dunham. As a result, bickering ensued across the green, with Wade, wanting the land all to himself, presumably hurling all sorts of insults and damnations at the Episcopalians. With the two congregations both laying claim to the land, however, there was little to calm the Sabbath until the freeholders finally replaced Wade with Reverend John Pierson, son of Yale University founder Abraham Pierson, in 1715. At that point, they duly snapped away use of the Kirk Green from Wade—to whom they had promised it for only as long as he remained the town minister—and showed him where he could shove his "convictions."

By now, Woodbridge wasn't quite the backwater it had once been, so ministers were becoming harder to get rid of than to come by. Perhaps this explains Wade's preternatural tenacity to the point of obnoxiousness: Woodbridge was indeed becoming prime real estate as an important commercial and communications hub, encompassing—as it then did—both Rahway and Elizabeth, through which the King's Highway ran, and also offering the most direct route across the Arthur Kill to Staten Island from its docks in what is now Sewaren. Consequently, the Presbyterians had no difficulty finding a replacement for Pierson when a squabble with his parishioners led him to relinquish his post at age sixty-three; soon thereafter, he was replaced, in 1755, by Nathaniel Whittaker, who oversaw the First Presbyterian Church's securing a royal charter from Governor Johnathan Belcher in 1756. And Whittaker, in turn, was replaced in 1761 with Reverend Azel Roe—a mix of firebrand, wit and corpulent lush who would win a permanent place in the town annals as a Revolutionary War hero before his tenure ended in 1815.

Still, Woodbridge's religious drama didn't end with the Presbyterians' settling down. Problems now arose among the Episcopalians, who also saw their share of ministerial shenanigans when Vaughn and Halliday began feuding. According to Dally, Halliday started complaining to the missionaries' home office about how the Episcopalians' Piscataway church remained incomplete because of Vaughn. This was fair enough, for it was the uppity Vaughn who had halted construction to insist on a brick church instead of the wooden one the congregation had originally contracted from one Mr. Barron. Because of this, however, Halliday ended up counting himself out of the mix after Vaughn and another missionary, a Mr. Talbot, conspired to lock him out of both the Woodbridge and Amboy services.

The official reason Vaughn and Talbot gave for dispossessing Halliday of his rectory at St. Peter's in Perth Amboy was that Halliday had supposedly taken a hardline position against the area's Quakers and against the supremacy of the Church of England in colonial governance.

When they first began meeting in town around 1711, Woodbridge's Episcopalians held services in the home of congregant Benjamin Dunham, son of miller Jonathan Dunham. *Public domain.*

The real reason, though, was likely that—as Halliday himself had complained—there was no salary at that point for any Episcopalian minister in New Jersey outside Elizabeth, whose rector received the mere thirty pounds sterling per year that Halliday and Vaughn must have been splitting up until then. Further, Halliday's sermons against the Quakers (if they actually occurred) hadn't won him many friends among the numerous powerful members of this sect in the colony's legislature. But, his accusing one Mr. George Willocks (or "Willoks") of misappropriating church funds became the straw that sent the proverbial camel to the emergency room: you see, as Ned C. Landsman points out in his *Scotland and Its First American Colony, 1683–1765,* Willocks was the well-connected son of a prominent Restoration-era Episcopalian minister in Kemnay Parish, Scotland. And, having immigrated to East Jersey in 1683 as land agent to Scottish proprietor Robert Gordon, Laird of Cluny, he had become one of the wealthiest landowners in Monmouth County. Moreover, Willocks had been a fervent Jacobite (one who favored the restoration of James II to the throne of England), so Halliday's complaints against Willocks—which Vaughn characterized as "base and barbarous treatment"—crossed the politically powerful older gentlemen not just publically but personally.

The end result, then, was that the minister had made himself so singularly odious to everyone that, according to Dally, even Governor Hunter referred to him as "that wretch" and mused that he wished "the country could get rid of [Halliday] at any [cost]." Like the Presbyterians' infamous Wade, though, he clung on, continuing as Piscataway's Episcopal minister until 1718, when he quit New Jersey completely. This left the Woodbridge, Piscataway and Amboy Episcopalians without a minister for four years until, in 1722, Reverend William Skinner took up the church's reins.

If anyone was something like the Episcopalians' version of the legendary Reverend Roe, it was Reverend Skinner, who served as minister of the Woodbridge and Piscataway congregations and rector of St. Peter's in Perth Amboy until his death at age seventy in 1758. Of course, to be sure, he wasn't exactly fond of his situation when he first took over: as per Dally, he bemoaned how the partially built church on Woodbridge's Kirk Green was little more than "clap boards nailed together in a very sorry manner" and how his fifty Woodbridge parishioners were mostly Dissenters—a subsect of Episcopalians who, like the Presbyterians, refused to recognize England's monarch as head of the church. However, under his guidance, in 1754, the Woodbridge congregation completed its first true church at the site of today's Trinity Episcopal Church. And, though he wasn't a Revolutionary War hero like Roe, there is evidence he served as a preacher in what historians today term the "First Great Awakening," a period of religious revival and rethinking in the United States in the mid-eighteenth century. For, as Dally records, Skinner, as a man in his sixties, complained about trudging across the Raritan River in the summer of 1749 to preach at some location along the South River near modern-day Sayreville. Such open-air ministries were a hallmark of the First Great Awakening. And so, despite his curmudgeonly grumbling, Skinner may have been something of a revolutionary in the tradition of John Edwards, believing that every spiritual experience was personal and, most radically, that all people—including slaves—were equal in the eyes of God.

Breaking New Ground: Woodbridge as It Appeared in the Colonial Period

As mentioned at the start of this chapter, if there was ever a "wooden bridge," it probably stood in Woodbridge, England. But, naturally, there was an actual wooden bridge in our own Woodbridge; in fact, there were dozens of them—for what else other than wood could the town's first residents have used for bridge-building? According to Joseph Dally, the town's first wooden bridge was erected over Papiak Creek (the original name for Woodbridge Creek), probably near where today's Port Reading Avenue and Trinity Lane meet behind the First Presbyterian Church. Hence, though there was never an eponymous bridge per se, we might think of this original bridge as the closest thing to it, since it would have been one of the first landmarks a visitor would see traveling into Woodbridge from its most common seventeenth-century entry and departure points—its ports and docks in Sewaren.

That brings us to another point about Woodbridge as it looked when its original settlers first built it: it originally consisted of some thirty thousand acres encompassing land on which the modern towns of Carteret (originally Blazing Star), Rahway (Spanktown, Leesville and Bridgetown), Metuchen and Edison (Bonhamtown) now sit, as well as the areas that would become today's communities of Avenel, Colonia, Fords (Slingtown), Hopelawn, Iselin, Keasbey, Menlo Park Terrace, Port Reading, Sewaren and Woodbridge Proper. In other words, Woodbridge was much, *much*

Woodbridge's Presbyterian cemetery is one of New Jersey's oldest; it originated as part of the Kirk Green, land apportioned for church use in the township's 1669 charter. *Zeete.*

larger at the time of its charter and, interestingly enough, faced eastward in those days, toward Staten Island. Thus, the entrance to the old meetinghouse, where the First Presbyterian Church now stands, would have been on the opposite side of the building. And, because the Presbyterian and Episcopalian churches hadn't yet been built, the next landmark worth noting would have been Jonathan Dunham's gristmill, once adjacent to Trinity Episcopal's rectory.

As for the gristmill, specifically, it was built in 1670 on the portion of the town greens where Trinity Episcopal Church now stands, after the town granted Dunham thirty pounds and all the sod he needed to dam the Papiak for the project. According to Dally, Dunham's milling toll was one-sixteenth of the ground grain produced by the milling process, and it is said that Dunham could turn one bag of grain into two bags of flour—probably a gross exaggeration, considering that, in those days, a miller wasn't usually a town's favorite inhabitant, as necessary as he might have been.

Built with imported Dutch brick around 1700, the Dunham House is not only Trinity Episcopal Church's rectory but the town's longest-standing home still in use. *Zeete.*

Indeed, millers were known to frequently swindle their customers, so perhaps Woodbridge's nineteenth-century historian misheard the local saying, and it was instead, "He'll grind one bag of grain *for* two bags of flour." Or, maybe, as was common practice back to the medieval period, Dunham often added chalk dust to his flour, thus yielding that extra bag. In any event, though, Dunham's epitaph was probably more backhand than compliment, since little love was ever lost between a town and its miller when milling was still a thing. Nor should this surprise us if it's true, since Dunham was reportedly quite well-off by the end of his life, allowing him to spare no expense on his house, building it from immensely expensive, imported Dutch bricks in a town where brickmaking was the primary industry.

What's more, Dunham himself was probably at least as interesting as the longstanding landmark his mill would afford him. You see, buried in Walter Meuly's history of neighboring Piscataway is a Jonathan Dunham of Salem, Massachusetts, who ran afoul of Puritan authorities in 1622, when he was convicted of slandering one John Godfrey. Reportedly, what earned Dunham his stay in the clink was his saying of Godfrey, "Is this witch on this side of Boston gallows yet?"

Now, to be sure, there is no evidence in the source materials that the Dunham of Woodbridge and the Dunham of Salem and Piscataway were one and the same. But how many Jonathan Dunhams could have possibly been roaming the Woodbridge area in the seventeenth century? And, anyhow, it's nice to imagine our Dunham beside the fireplace in his big, brick house, feeling vindicated in his old age by his success and still more than willing to call that Godfrey fellow a witch again, given a do-over. At the very least, this scenario is plausible considering that many of Woodbridge's early residents were Quakers and Baptists from Portsmouth, New Hampshire, on the Piscataqua River, which was then owned by the Massachusetts Bay Company. In fact, it is by no means a stretch to think Jonathan Dunham (who was just twenty-two years old when he was sent up for slander) decided to follow some of his prison mates south years later. Who wouldn't, after all, want to make themselves scarce, what with Salem hanging four Quakers in 1654 and Boston passing a law against Baptists as late as a decade later?

Indeed, we must remember that the sectarian hate rife in Massachusetts would not reach its apex until the Salem witch trials of 1692. So many of Woodbridge's early town fathers were likely refugees from New England. Those Puritans, after all, didn't mess around when it came to religious intolerance. As per Meuly, for example, the infamous Puritan firebrand Cotton Mather once suggested seizing a ship spiriting William Penn and one hundred Quakers away from Boston, to sell the whole kaboodle as a "'lot of heretics and malignants,' in Barbados, 'where slaves fetch good prices in rum and sugar.'"

At any rate, though, returning to our brief description of the town as it existed prior to the American Revolution, we find the first road in Woodbridge was built using the same slash-and-burn techniques the Lenape had used to flush out deer and was a combination of what are now Trinity Lane and Port Reading Avenue. It passed the "Kirk" (or Church) Green before continuing over Woodbridge Creek, which, it should also be noted, was large enough—until the Salamander Brick Works was built in the mid-nineteenth century—to accommodate the anchorage of shipping vessels.

This photo of Trinity Episcopal's churchyard shows the millstone of Woodbridge's first mill, which Jonathan Dunham built near the Kirk Green in the 1670s. *Public domain.*

Until a 1906 charter made it Roosevelt, New Jersey, Carteret and its gorgeous waterfront on the Arthur Kill were known as the Woodbridge neighborhood of Blazing Star. *Jared Kofsky.*

In 1670, then, additional roads were laid out, including today's Freeman Street, Rahway Avenue, Amboy Avenue and Main Street, as well as what is now State Street in Sewaren. Dally also tells us Pierce's Landing stood at the northern mouth of Woodbridge Creek, where Motiva Enterprises now stands, near the site of Boynton Beach, while Vanquilion's Landing (aka "the Old Stone Dock"), which was named for the first provincial surveyor general, stood directly across the mouth of the creek.

Other colonial landings included Bacon's Landing, Cornfield Landing (later "Cutter's Dock") and Cortland's Landing, supposedly located on Smith's Creek, where the colony's first sawmill stood. All in all, then, with the exception of the colonials' many docks, which have since been replaced with industrial ports and factories, the depth of the Papiack and the general orientation of town, early Woodbridge would look remarkably familiar to modern eyes. Indeed, reading through a 1748 diary entry by Professor Peter Kalm, a Swedish botanist who passed through Woodbridge less than a century after its founding, we might even recognize some of the town's older homes, such as the Aaron Dunn House—which was built in 1685 and stands at what is now 12 Freeman Street—and the Cross Keys Tavern—which was built in 1740 by Woodbridge's first postmaster, John Manning, at what is now 142 North James Street:

> *Woodbridge is a small village in a plain, consisting of a few houses; we stopped here to rest our horses a little; The houses were most of them built of boards; the walls had covering of shingles on the outside; these shingles were round at one end and all of a length in each row; some of the houses had an Italian roof, but the greatest part had roofs with pediments; most of them were covered with shingles.*

CHAPTER II

SETTING BOUNDARIES

Border Disputes, Land Wars and the Sonmans Affair

A s Woodbridge was coming together, several other settlements were springing up, too. Among these, its relationships with nearby Piscataway and "Amboy Point" (later Perth Amboy) became the most contentious because of boundary disputes.

The earliest of these began in the summer of 1669, when the first instance in a series of longstanding colonial troubles with Piscataway is noted on July 6 in the Woodbridge Town Book. According to Joseph Dally, the area where Piscataway now sits was originally a Lenape village until the Gilman family moved to the area. Thus, when Governor Carteret granted one hundred square miles between the Raritan and Rahway Rivers to John Pike and Daniel Pierce and Associates of Newbury on December 11, 1666, it probably wasn't Carteret's to give. Indeed, we know from Dally that Carteret didn't buy the land between Piscataway and Woodbridge from the Lenape Conamackamack, Capatamin and Thingorawis until 1677. It is little wonder, then, that Piscataway Township wasn't fully incorporated until 1798, after the American Revolution, or that its sketchy boundaries became grounds for a dispute with Woodbridge.

However, what is definitely known of the dispute's origins is that it began with Daniel Pierce and Associates selling a third of its land for thirty pounds to John Martin, Charles Gilman, Hugh Dunn and Hopewell Hull just a week after Carteret's grant—a move that, in his *History of Piscataway Township*, Walter Meuly says must have been prearranged between the governor and the land speculators, because Pierce and Associates had agreed to settle forty families on the Piscataway territory as a stipulation for the governor's assent. Of course, several of the purchasers from Pierce and Associates, like John Pike, were also Woodbridge settlers. So, the confusion over where Woodbridge ended and Piscataway began probably started as a question of where to draw a township line in the middle of contiguous properties.

And yet, there may be another hint as to its origins in Piscataway's name itself. You see, while Dally speculates that it is a Munsee word meaning "it's getting dark," Meuly probably comes closer to the mark when he points out that the town's second wave of settlers—many of them eventually Woodbridge men as well, including Benjamin Hull, John Gilman, Robert Dennis and John Smith—arrived in 1668 and hailed from a settlement near the Piscataqua, a tidal river in New Hampshire. Consequently, Piscataway's name might not be Munsee at all, but Abenaki, and it might instead mean "strong tides." What's more, land feuds might just be in the blood of folks from those parts, for the states of Maine and New Hampshire carried on one of the nation's longest land disputes from 1866 to 2002, when the Supreme Court finally decided a lawsuit over five artificial islands the U.S. Navy had created in the Piscataqua during the Civil War.

At any rate, in 1669, Captain John Pike, Thomas Bloomfield Sr., Stephen Kent Sr. and Samuel Moore were sent as representatives to Piscataway to hash out why its residents had torn down boundary markers set up by the surveyor general to divide Woodbridge and Piscataway, and whatever was said, Piscataway's settlers apparently continued to tear down the markers. Then, on August 16, 1669, Woodbridge sent the same committee to complain to Governor Carteret but still got no satisfaction in the matter.

In fact, the troubles with Piscataway would continue throughout the colonial period, with a July 2, 1674, town meeting mentioning that Daniel Dutton and John Gilman of Piscataway were filing suit against Woodbridge for the upland and meadows between the towns. The lawsuit was filed during the brief Dutch takeover of New Jersey the previous year, so it was dropped after Carteret was restored to office. But there is some chance that Piscataway was in the right, since Woodbridge resident and colonial surveyor general under Carteret, Robert Vanquilion, was implicated in fraudulent activity in 1682—after Carteret's government was replaced by that of East Jersey governor Robert Barclay. According to Dally, Barclay's administration found discrepancies in the paperwork of Carteret's secretary of the province, one Captain Vickers, and, subsequently, Vanquilion was charged with ignoring proprietary concessions when making surveys and with doing so sans dates or warrants from the proper authorities.

An order to confiscate Vanquilion's records was then issued, and he was also jailed by Moore on March 21, 1683. But, two days later, Vanquilion denied in court that he'd ever had such paperwork, in response to which, on March 26, 1683, the colonial House of Deputies passed a bill barring Vanquilion and Samuel Edsall from ever holding public office again. Dally speculates that this is because Edsall helped destroy the paperwork in question, though certainly, if Vanquilion was engaged in unsavory behavior vis-a-vis Piscataway, his surveys would have benefitted his neighbors in Woodbridge, including the same high sheriff instructed to arrest him. So, as for *who* might have destroyed said paperwork—if it ever even existed in the first place—plenty of Woodbridge residents would have had more than ample motive and opportunity to lend a hand as the surveyor moldered in jail.

Joseph Dally, the only historian to record this seemingly minor incident of Woodbridge history, doesn't provide much more information regarding Vanquilion's arrest. So, its import must necessarily remain in the realm of conjecture. Key, however, are the charges that Vanquilion hadn't recorded the proprietors' concessions or dated his deeds, and this smacks of a connection to the trouble over Governor Richard Nicolls's grants. After all, Carteret did make some effort to honor Nicolls's premature land grants as long as the deeded freeholders paid their quitrents. If the concessions in question, then, were those to the quitrent-paying holders of Nicolls's deeds and, further, Vanquilion had neglected to include the dates of original acquisition in his surveys, his actions might have contributed to the dissatisfaction of New Jersey's growing antiproprietary political faction, which had already embroiled the colony in so many uprisings and riots under Carteret that the original proprietors sold their shares—thus leading to the change of government and Vanquilion's fall from grace. That Governor Barclay's administration could have had another reason for pursuing action against Vanquilion so soon after the colony had changed hands is hard to imagine. But, without firmer evidence (the kind Vanquilion supposedly never had), this explanation is no more than speculation.

Still, whatever the truth of Vanquilion's involvement, New Jersey's antiproprietary movement is important in the case of Woodbridge's boundary dispute with Piscataway because it was the competing land claims created by the Nicolls grants that would stymie attempts to institute town boundaries throughout the first century after Woodbridge's founding. In the case of the Woodbridge-Piscataway dispute, the matter took roughly thirty years to iron out, and it wasn't until 1701 that Woodbridge's freeholders could finally hold the first of their seven land divisions. The dispute with Perth Amboy, on the other hand, was far more complicated and took much longer to resolve.

MAKING THE POINT, PART I: THE BORDER DISPUTE WITH PERTH AMBOY AND THE LAND WARS

A Scottish enclave at its inception, Perth Amboy was first settled in 1665, immediately after Governor Philip Carteret's arrival, and the first governor intended it to be one of two deep-water ports in New Jersey (the other being Elizabeth). Its name comes from the Lenape "Ambo," meaning "point," and perhaps because of the redundancy of its original name, "Ambo Point," it was redubbed "Perth Amboy" in honor of the Earl of Perth after he became a proprietor. The city would develop into one of the major ports in the entire colony and, in fact, was one of New Jersey's most important slave markets until, in 1842, its indoor marketplace burned down. Regrettably, despite its advantages to New Jersey's first English colonists, it never rivaled New York City, which the Dutch had already developed as a seaport to the point that the Big Apple's primacy as the colonies' largest city was never in doubt.

Now, to be sure, because it's less than five miles from Woodbridge, Perth Amboy has always figured into Woodbridge history. And, of course, as the colonial capital following New Jersey's split into East and West Jersey, Perth Amboy also exerted political power over its neighbor to the north. But, as far as the boundary dispute goes, there is barely a mention of it in Woodbridge's annals until a committee—consisting of John Bloomfield and John and Thomas Pike—was formed to divide the two towns on the eve of New Jersey's reunification in 1701.

This attempt was confounded, however, by one of the colony's major movers and shakers, prominent Perth Amboy resident and proprietor Peter Sonmans. Subsequently, the dividing line between the towns would become one of Woodbridge's first major court cases when, in 1709, John Pike sued Sonmans on behalf of the town's freeholders for laying claim to several acres of common land in Woodbridge. A whole generation would eventually pass before the case against Sonmans was settled in 1737 by the New Jersey Supreme Court. This lengthy wait came about not only because of Sonmans's political connectedness as a proprietor but because of the general politics of the era. Sonmans, you see, was a key player in the ongoing attempts by many Jersey residents to overthrow proprietary rule, and as such, he had allies among Woodbridge's freeholders.

But the root of these issues lies even deeper in the colony's history, long before Sonmans became a thorn in Woodbridge's side. In fact, to some extent, it had to do with New Jersey's attempts to establish a boundary between itself and New York. You see, many of those who had agitated for an end to proprietary rule in New Jersey had been the same men who'd purchased tracts of land from the Lenape with Governor Richard Nicolls's assent. To express their discontent, many had refused to pay the quitrents Carteret imposed. Thus, tempers flared when the October 25, 1670, Woodbridge town meeting saw the freeholders reading an order from Carteret to confiscate and reallocate the land of antiproprietary colonists who hadn't paid their quitrents.

Woodbridge residents who, according to Joseph Dally, possibly lost their land after Carteret's order included Robert Rogers, Daniel Robins, Isaac Tappan, Thomas Adams, John Averill, Johnathan Bishop, James Clawson (also Clarkson), Jonathan Dennis, Hopewell Hull and Thomas Pike, as their names don't appear in the 1685 landowner rolls. Additionally, Surveyor General Robert Vanquilion received a warrant from Carteret directing Woodbridge to divide the remaining unowned land despite opposition—this likely referred to dividing up the confiscated land among the town's taxpaying settlers. Regardless of whose land was confiscated, what's important about this episode is that it fanned already-simmering flames that would erupt two years later in a series of riots in Elizabethtown, Shrewsbury and Middletown.

The Elizabethtown riot was what sparked the state of disorder that spread throughout the rest of the colony, and it started on May 14, 1672, when a group of antiproprietary colonists rallied in the then-capital, claiming to be the colony's legal legislature. The situation in Elizabethtown got so bad that Governor Carteret fled to England, sparking further riots in Shrewsbury and Middletown. However, the insurrectionists' actions actually backfired once Carteret arrived in Britain and reported what had happened to the proprietors. In response, the Duke of York sent a letter to New York's then-Governor Lovelace, commanding him to disavow the riots and deem the Nicolls grants void. According to Troeger and McEwen, meanwhile, Lord Berkeley and Sir George Carteret were experiencing financial problems anyhow, and Berkeley became so disgusted with the additional stress of the rioting that on March 18, 1673, he sold his shares to Quakers John Fenwick and Edward Byllinge for just a little over the equivalent of $1 million in today's money, splitting the colony into East Jersey and West Jersey.

With the chaos in New York and New Jersey leaving both colonies open to attack, the Dutch took advantage of the situation, and their fleet appeared in New York harbor not long after Berkeley sold his shares. Suffice it to say, this is pertinent to our overall tale because Peter Sonmans was Dutch and so no doubt enjoyed some favoritism from the Dutch authorities after they captured New York City in July 1673. In contrast, although they generally allowed all of New Jersey's colonists freedom of conscience and the retention of existing lands, when Woodbridge fell under Dutch rule later that summer, the Dutch harassed several of the town's inhabitants, including Samuel Moore and Vanquilion. Moore got on the wrong side of Dutch East Jersey schout (i.e., governor) John Ogden for refusing, as Carteret's marshal, to hand over a warrant for a bail bond in his possession. He was convicted of the charges after appealing to the Dutch authorities in "New Orange" (what the Dutch redubbed New York City) on May 26, 1674. Vanquilion, meanwhile, was tried for sedition against the Dutch and banished outright.

And yet, despite the restoration of English rule to the newly separated East and West New Jersey colonies in 1674 and the return of Philip Carteret as governor of East Jersey, colonial governance became even more unstable. For, although the colonists who had rioted just two years earlier chose not to reinitiate their exemption claims and paid their quitrents of one-half to one pence per acre (today, equivalent to roughly thirteen to twenty-six cents per acre), a new New York governor had been appointed—the fussy and domineering Edmund Andros. Andros and Carteret were hardly each other's biggest fans. In fact, at one point, Andros attempted to take over East Jersey in what we would now call a "coup," sending a unit of troops across the Hudson on April 7, 1680, to intimidate Carteret.

Interestingly, as there were more troops guarding Elizabeth than he'd bargained for, Andros instead had Carteret kidnapped and secreted across the Hudson that night. Carteret subsequently spent the rest of the summer locked in a New York prison while Andros attempted to persuade the East Jersey assembly that the proprietors had put him in charge of both colonies. Naturally, the assembly found the New York governor's claims preposterous and struck down a proposal to join New York and East Jersey under one government, waylaying Andros's takeover until the rightful government was restored in March 1681. But this was not before proprietor Sir George Carteret (cousin of Philip) died on January 14, 1680.

Following Sir George's death, his share of the colony was sold to Pennsylvania founder William Penn and East Jersey's first deputy governor, Thomas Rudyard, in 1682. Thus, poor, bedeviled Philip was replaced by absentee Governor Robert Barclay, and Barclay, in turn, appointed Rudyard, who arrived to relieve Carteret in November 1682. Soon after his ouster, Philip Carteret suffered a precipitous physical decline, leading to his death in December 1682, so the question of his restoration to the governorship in place of Andros was obviously moot. Even so, Woodbridge's town fathers were undoubtedly proud of their resistance to the Andros regime; for instance, they'd refused to send Andros the names of men who could serve as small-claims judges until, finally, they grudgingly complied under threat of reprisal on August 31, 1680. This was despite the antiproprietary sentiments of some freeholders, who likely hoped Andros would retain control and restore their Piscataway Nicolls grants. When they instead received word, in 1682, that Penn and others had purchased Sir George Carteret's shares and, in 1684, that these new owners had formed the Board of Proprietors of the Eastern Division of New Jersey, it certainly couldn't have done much to quell the simmering dissent.

To combat this tension—which wasn't the only instance of antiproprietary fervor in the British colonies—Parliament did try to limit proprietors' governing power as part of its Navigation Act of 1696. This law instituted the Board of Trade in London and invested it with exclusive power to appoint governors for proprietary colonies (with the consent of the monarch, of course). Moreover, as Gordon Bond points out in his book *Wicked Woodbridge & Crazy Carteret*, the new law also forced proprietors to enter a one-thousand-pound-sterling bond for whomever the board appointed—likely with an eye toward defraying the expense Parliament would incur if said governor ended up a train wreck and troops had to be called in. This only made matters worse, though, because East Jersey's Board of Proprietors failed to pay the bond when the Board of Trade selected West Jersey governor Jeremiah Basse as governor of East Jersey. Thus, when Basse assumed office in East Jersey in 1697, he didn't have the proper credentials, and his governorship therefore only served to further agitate the antiproprietary colonists.

Basse found his most powerful enemy in Lewis Morris, whom the governor had dismissed from the governor's council when he took office. And, as the Board of Proprietors took no action to mollify the former counselor, Morris was incensed. Ironically, Morris was a proprietor himself and had previously defended proprietary rights as a justice under the prior governor, Andrew Hamilton. However, following his dismissal under Basse, he became a friend

Before becoming governor in 1715, Lewis Morris was the ringleader of the Anti-Proprietary Party and even found himself locked in the Woodbridge jail on charges of treason. *Public domain.*

of the antiproprietary movement and, in 1698, burst into a hearing of the Court of Common Right as Basse was bringing it to order. Brandishing a sword, Morris reportedly challenged Basse's right—again, without the proper credentials—to take any action in East Jersey, including calling a court to order. That the outraged Morris was summarily arrested and jailed for this only served to inflame his allies.

Consequently, then, Morris went on an anti-Basse tear when Basse became vulnerable later that year. The circumstances of this reversal originated in Basse's attempts to finally drag both Jerseys out of New York's shadow and to further develop Perth Amboy as a major port. You see, at that point, the Board of Trade still favored New York as the northern colonies' primary port, so it required all ships entering or leaving the smaller surrounding ports, like Perth Amboy, to stop in New York harbor and pay a customs fee. Basse and the proprietors contended this was unnecessary and unfair, because New York could not impose taxes on jurisdictions that its legislature didn't govern. In a bid to force the issue and have a case brought before the High Court at Westminster, Basse and his allies devised a plan to challenge New York's dominance once and for all: Basse ordered a sloop, the *Hester*, owned by him and his brother-in-law, John Lofting, to flout paying customs fees at New York harbor by putting in and unloading its cargo directly at Perth Amboy. When New York responded by forcibly seizing the *Hester* in the Perth Amboy harbor as its crew loaded a new cargo of barrel staves, the first part of Basse's plan came to fruition. However, the second part—that of bringing a court case against New York—became much harder to realize.

The reason for Basse's difficulty at this juncture was that, first and foremost, several of the *Hester*'s New Jersey crewmen had suffered injuries in the sloop's seizure, and they and their captain were being detained in New York until the customs fee was paid—all in the name of Basse's scheme. This certainly didn't sit well with the East Jersey Assembly, which had just seen power shift when antiproprietary assemblymen won elections to several seats in its lower chamber. So, when he requested funds to pursue a case against New York governor Richard Coote for the seizure, Basse found himself confounded by the assembly's new speaker, John Harriman—who was, in fact, an advocate for unifying New York and East Jersey. As a result, the situation with the *Hester* dragged on until an ailing Harriman stepped down in 1699. By then, the captain and crew of the *Hester* had been rotting in New York jail cells for the better part of a year. Thus, when the assembly finally did vote to give Basse the 675 pounds sterling he needed to mount his lawsuit, his blatant attempt to play puppetmaster with the lives of others only fueled antiproprietary sentiments in East Jersey.

Matters came to a head when Basse's old enemy, Morris, began traveling around East Jersey fanning the flames of the colonists' resentment. He reminded them that Basse wasn't even actually the governor, because he had never received the requisite credentials from the Board of Trade and the King; Basse, he asserted, was no more than a tyrant, and the sooner the colonists could oust him, the better off they'd be. In response, Basse considered fleeing to London while preparing for his upcoming court case. Instead, he arrested Morris and his fellow ringleader George Willocks—the very same George Willocks whom Woodbridge's Reverend Halliday would later accuse of misappropriating church funds—and imposed a 300-pound-sterling bond on each man against further agitation, with the additional threat that he'd charge the pair with treason if they didn't fall in line. Realizing Basse was already foundering politically, both Morris and Willocks refused to post their bonds, and they subsequently found themselves—along with a third man, Thomas Gordon—indicted for high crimes in inciting the colonists against the government.

The charges were serious—*dead* serious; treason was a capital offense. So, when Morris and Willocks were imprisoned in the Woodbridge jail, their supporters could hardly have been expected to stand idly by. A sizable number of colonists had already begun to ignore proprietary rule and all claims to the proprietors' governmental authority. Much like many of their modern descendants, they felt it was their duty to defy unjust laws that trampled their God-given liberties as Englishmen and Scotsmen. In fact, antiproprietary fervor was so high that no one would stop an attempt to free Morris and Willocks. Anyone who would stand in the way would become a traitor in the eyes of his neighbors. Such reasoning was rife, especially in Elizabeth, where the decades-long "land wars" had begun because of the Nicolls grants. As a result, between 2:00 and 4:00 a.m. on May 13, 1677—the day after Morris and Willocks were imprisoned—a mass of Elizabeth residents took up "staves and other weapons" and marched in force on Woodbridge under the leadership of Isaac Whitehead.

Demanding East Jersey be brought under Crown rule, the rioters beat any proprietary officers they caught and burst into the town jail with a battering ram, freeing everyone inside. When the Basse administration learned of the riot the next day, all they found in place of Morris and Willocks was the following note (via Bond) written by Willocks and signed by both men:

> We are now able (God be thank'd) to treat with you any way you think fit; if you had valued either your own or the Welfare of ye Government, your procedures had been more calm. Your day is not yet out & it is yet in your Power to follow the things that make for peace, & if you do not, at your door lye the consequences. Our friends will not suffer us to be put upon.

Basse did the only thing he could under the circumstances and ordered Middlesex high sheriff and Woodbridge resident Nathaniel Fitz Randolph to apprehend Morris and Willocks on May 16, 1699. By then, though, the governor's two nemeses were already on the lam, and as for Fitz Randolph, the sheriff was himself an outspoken member of the antiproprietary faction, so the governor's order presumably fell on deaf ears. In response, Basse did, to be sure, relieve Fitz Randolph of his station, but to no avail. As the very same council from which he'd ejected Morris met in Perth Amboy to discuss its next steps, the incorrigible Willocks sailed a sloop into the colonial capital's harbor and fired the ship's cannon at the counselors' chambers. Apparently, no one was hurt, but Willocks's message was clear: the antiproprietary faction would not let up.

In a last-ditch bid to retain power, Basse's government threatened those involved in the Woodbridge riot, but nothing ever came of these threats, since, at that point, Basse and the proprietors were too politically weak to garner support for a prosecution. Amid the general disorder that ensued, Basse was recalled to London and replaced by his predecessor, Andrew Hamilton. But, when Hamilton attempted to call the next session of the East Jersey Assembly to order, the proprietors' supporters demanded the new governor's credentials of royal sponsorship. Of course, as these assemblymen well knew, Hamilton had been too recently reinstated to have received these documents from Britain. But, even so, since the reinstated governor couldn't produce his credentials, they refused to acknowledge his authority and dissolved the assembly.

In Woodbridge, meanwhile, minutes from the town's meetings reveal that, due to the apparent popularity of the antiproprietary cause, the freeholders were, by and large, loyal to Hamilton, having voted by general consent (i.e., a vote of not just the freeholders but of all the inhabitants present) at the May 6, 1700, town meeting to order their own representative in the East Jersey assembly to acknowledge the governor. This vote might have been what incited Woodbridge's nonvoting residents (i.e., those who didn't own land, including those who had had it taken) to riot again after the May assembly in Elizabethtown had broken up and chaos once more overtook East Jersey. But unlike with the jailbreak riot the previous year, when the rioters attacked the Woodbridge jail, this time, they broke into the "King's Store," or munitions magazine and treasury, and looted its gunpowder.

And so it was that the rebellion continued with another general riot throughout both East and West Jerseys in 1701, at which point the proprietors relinquished governmental control of the colonies to the Crown.

On April 17, 1702, Queen Anne accepted ownership of the reunited colony of New Jersey, appointing her cousin Edward Hyde, Lord Cornbury, as joint royal governor for both New York and New Jersey. The hopes of the queen and the proprietors, we might imagine, were that this move would end New Jersey's land wars once and for all. But, as history shows, the newly strengthened antiproprietary movement and the turbulence it would cause in Woodbridge and elsewhere were just beginning.

Making the Point, Part II: Sonmans-Stelle and the Blind Tax

As it turned out, Lord Cornbury would become one of New Jersey's most "colorful" governors—and well ahead of his time, as he was infamous in his day for cross-dressing. Still, of far more importance than what Cornbury wore was how his behavior as governor nearly tore the newly reunited colony of New Jersey apart. Described by Troeger and McEwen as bigoted, unintelligent and greedy, Cornbury rarely left Manhattan unless goaded by his royal cousin to quell yet another bout of New Jersey unrest. Worse, he banned printing presses in New Jersey during his tenure in a bid to stem dissent.

How all this came to pass is a matter rarely discussed in local histories but one in which Woodbridge plays a central role. It began with the antiproprietary colonists, who, even with the colony now under crown rule, were still so dissatisfied with the status quo that Cornbury discovered accepting New Jersey's governorship meant practically walking into a lion's den. For evidence of this, we need look no further than a letter Cornbury wrote Colonel Robert Dudley just one month after the end of the first New Jersey Assembly session he presided over: "I should not have been so long writing to your Excellency but that I was detained in Jersey a considerable time longer than I expected; I find that Country much divided, but I hope in a little time to compose matters there."

At issue were two essential facts that Robert Quary, surveyor general for all of British North America, pointed out to the Board of Trade: (1) the East Jersey and West Jersey assemblies had been ruled by minorities of Scottish and Quaker colonists, respectively, and (2) following reunification, these factions had quickly built an alliance. The only thing underpinning Scottish-Quaker power, Cornbury knew, was Queen Anne's directive that representatives to the assembly be chosen generally rather than on a county-by-county basis. Undoing the queen's directive would be a tall order, especially because of the Quakers, who were politically well-connected back in London. Cornbury also realized he would somehow have to change the political landscape, because otherwise, these two minority factions would make themselves increasingly unpopular, further undermining the colony's stability.

Ultimately, all of this has to do with Peter Sonmans because he, along with several other members of Cornbury's assembly, was actively seeking the same ends as the governor, although for different reasons and through different tactics. The governor's motivations for pursuing county-based assembly elections were, as Daniel Weeks explains, to improve the colony's economic and civil stability, while leaders of the antiproprietary faction in the assembly were mostly concerned with dislodging the proprietor-supporting Quakers from the House of Representatives, having the Nicolls grants restored and ending the quitrent system. In other words, the antiproprietary faction didn't want to pay taxes—a complaint that should sound familiar to any contemporary political observer.

The leading antiproprietary assemblymen, in addition to Sonmans, included Richard Saltar and his brother-in-law John Bowne Jr., both of whom attended the November–December 1703 session of the legislature in Perth Amboy to protest what they saw as its illegal election. They were, therefore, conveniently on hand for Cornbury to schmooze, backchanneling through Quary, who was also present as a member of New Jersey's Colonial Council. Soon thereafter, then, Saltar and Bowne began approaching other antiproprietary freeholders for contributions to a secret fund to help effect their desired ends. This collection became known as the "Blind Tax" due to how Saltar and Bowne resisted disclosing the purpose of the collection to those who contributed. It actually consisted of two funds: the first was to pay an attorney to fight the 1703 elections and prevent the colony's adoption of the Long Bill, which would have expanded proprietary power under the Crown, while the second was intended to provide the colony with an operations fund to keep things running after Cornbury dissolved the assembly and called for new elections.

Of course, few—if any—contributors to the funds understood this, because Saltar and Bowne were mum about it all. Indeed, according to one anecdote related by Weeks, when Middletown freeholder Edmund Dunham pressed for more information about how Saltar intended to use the five pounds sterling Dunham had donated, Saltar replied that it was for the

Known for his cross-dressing, intrigue and colonial mismanagement, Edward Hyde, Lord Cornbury, was New Jersey's first governor after its 1702 reunification under Crown rule. *Public domain.*

public good and that "there must be no questions asked." Consequently, the ultimate effect of these cloak-and-dagger tactics was that they made it seem as if Saltar and Bowne were using their positions as assemblymen to rip off colonists. So, when Saltar convened a meeting in Woodridge at the home of the recently deceased antiproprietary supporter Richard Powell in 1704, town leaders John Pike and Samuel Dennis sat in with not a little skepticism toward Saltar's intentions. Subsequently, at Woodbridge's March 28, 1706, town meeting, Dennis and Pike were also appointed to present the New Jersey Assembly with the town's grievances against Saltar and Bowne in the form of the following petition (republished by Joseph Dally):

> *Richard Saltar of the County of Monmouth in the said Province in the Latter end of the year 1703 or Beginning of the year 1704 Did at Woodbridge aforesaid by subtle and crafty words and cunning insinuations (and, as your Petitioner believes, with sinister ends) inform your Petitioner and Mr. Samuel Dennis together with other Inhabitants of Woodbridge that the said Province was groaning under insuperable burthens, viz. that*

the constitutions of the Qualifications of Electors and Members required to serve in the General Assembly was an Encroachment upon and destructive to the Liberties and Privileges of the Inhabitants of this Province; that the then Representatives of the General Assembly were Enemies to the Country; that the then Officers Civil and Military were such as were no friends to the Country and Obnoxious to the People; that the Titles of the Freeholders' lands were like to be called in question and either destroyed or become precarious for a Remedy, whereof the said Saltar did propose to your Petitioner and the said Samuel Dennis and others that if the Country (or the Eastern Division as your Petitioner understood him) would raise a sum of Seven or Eight hundred pounds which must be privately disposed of there could be obtained a dissolution of the then Assembly, a New one Elected, and the constitution of the qualifications of Electors and Representatives altered, the Lands confirmed, Particularly the Commons of Woodbridge, secured, such Officers turn'd out and in their Stead, such others appointed as might be pleasing to the People and such in Woodbridge as the Inhabitants of Woodbridge should nominate and that the money raised would only be Lent because an Act could be obtained from the next Assembly to Reimburse those generous Inhabitants that would advance the same. By which specious pretenses the said Saltar prevailed upon your Petitioner that he entered under a penal obligation of the sum of forty pounds for the payment of twenty pounds to Captain John Bowne a Member of your House according to the said Saltar's desire who did inform your Petitioner that the said Captain Bowne upon receipt of said obligation would readily advance the money since which time your Petitioner, perceiving the Fallacy and Deceit of the above said Pretenses was unwilling to pay the whole sum but though to his prejudice hath offered to compound with the said Bowne, provided he would make an abatement which he still refuseth to do but on the contrary threatens to put the said obligation in suit.

As this portion of the petition shows, Woodbridge's freeholders—officially, at least—thought Bowne and Saltar's Blind Tax was an excuse to extort money from unsuspecting colonists. If we believe, as Pike attests, that both Saltar and Bowne threatened to sue Pike for the twenty pounds sterling he had promised them, the two antiproprietary ringleaders certainly weren't making much of a case that they were doing otherwise. The reality is that we will probably never know if these threats were actually made, since Pike and Dennis might very well have been acting as pro-proprietary plants meant to undermine the Blind Tax project by misconstruing it as extortion. In any event, the majority of Woodbridge's leaders seem to have been united against Saltar and Bowne, explaining something of their ensuing trouble with Sonmans—whom antiproprietary leader William Dockwra was just putting forward, along with Daniel Coxe Jr., for a position on the colonial council even as Pike was swearing to his 1707 affidavit.

Sonmans, it should be noted, had been born in 1667 in Rotterdam, Holland, to prominent Dutch Quaker and William Penn ally Arent Sonmans and so had come to East Jersey in his youth as a natural ally to the proprietary faction, for his father had purchased a sizable proprietary share of East Jersey in 1682.

Perhaps the younger Sonmans had reasons for turning on his father's friends. Arent died as the result of a gunshot wound to his thigh when he was supposedly accosted by highwaymen at Stone Hole, near Stilton, Scotland, in August 1683, while living in Wallingford in East Lothian and visiting fellow proprietor Robert Barclay. The implications that his father's death might have been murder and that Barclay might have been in on the conspiracy can't have been lost on the young Peter, since Arent died among his fellow Quakers in Scotland, and the pro-proprietary factions in the 1707 New Jersey Assembly were Scottish and Quaker as well. We will never know whether the elder Sonmans's murder was staged by his supposed "friends"—or whether, at the very least, Peter Sonmans suspected that it was. In any event, Peter Sonmans could not have known much more than we do, because at the time of Arent's death, Peter was still in school.

Thus, Peter Sonmans and his sisters inherited their father's proprietary shares, and after matriculating at the University of Leyden to major in mathematics in 1684, Peter also received control of further shares belonging to his stepuncle, John Hancock of Wallingford. This gave the young Sonmans and his two sisters a total of five and a quarter proprietary shares in East Jersey, the largest holding within any one family, prompting the twenty-one-year-old Sonmans to move, in 1688, to Perth Amboy, where he resided off and on for the next twenty years.

PETER SONMANS SEEMS TO have kept to himself for the first decade or so after his move to Perth Amboy. When he does finally appear in the historical records, he may originally have been acting as a proprietary supporter following the collapse of Basse's government, as he, Dockwra and Saltar were involved in the political gambit to remove Governor Hamilton from office in 1701. As mentioned earlier, of course, this gamble would backfire on the pro-proprietary East Jersey assemblymen when the proprietary council voted to relinquish governmental control of the colony to Queen Anne. So fervent were Sonmans and his two co-conspirators, though, that they did manage to block Hamilton's bid to become New Jersey's first royal governor, instead throwing their weight behind sitting New York governor Cornbury. Yet, it might not have mattered to Sonmans whether he was advancing the proprietary or antiproprietary cause since, as Weeks explains, the Perth Amboy resident's real horse in the race was that he hoped to block his brother-in-law Joseph Olmstead, husband of his sister Rachel and a Hamilton supporter, from claiming a greater share of the Sonmans family's East Jersey holdings. In other words, his motivations were simple self-interest and an apparent disregard for whether proprietors like himself had any role in the colony's government.

Why Sonmans, a proprietor himself, opposed the pro-proprietary Scottish-Quaker alliance in the assembly is truly a mystery. If the surviving records are any indication, his only true ally was himself, so you would think he'd want to preserve his portion of the annual quitrents. Apparently, Sonmans was such an enigma in his own time that it is nearly impossible to discern his motives to this day. In 1703, for instance, he wrote the Earl of Nottingham to accuse Provincial Secretary Basse of leaving England to flee outstanding debts and of doing such a bad job as East Jersey's governor that Basse's appointment as secretary would only exacerbate disorder in the colony. Sonmans's ultimate purpose in making these allegations may have been that he wanted the position of provincial secretary for himself, as revealed in the very same letter. How he could have been so shortsighted as to not see that he was undermining his own position as a proprietor (since Basse was pro-proprietary) is anyone's guess. Perhaps the reason, as per a letter to the earl from Basse himself, was that Sonmans made such scathing accusations because he owed the former governor money and had refused to pay. Nor, in the end, might Basse's response to Sonmans's accusations have been far from the truth, for Basse ended up winning the battle for Nottingham's favor and served as secretary until 1715.

What is certain, however, is that by 1707, when Dockwra was putting Sonmans forward for a colonial councillorship, Sonmans was practically broke and on shaky ground as a proprietor, with his sisters (and their husbands) having wrested control of the family's shares. This was pointed out as part of Sir Thomas Lane's objection, on behalf of the West Jersey Society, to Dockwra's nominating Sonmans, and it also figured into a letter Lane wrote Queen Anne in which he calls Sonmans "'a person who [had] so ill managed his own private affairs, and been guilty of so much injustice to [the Queen's] subjects'" that his appointment to the council would be anathema to the colony in general. That Sonmans ultimately did receive his councillorship by parrying Lane's aspersions with a confirmation from the master of rolls that he had retained his five and a quarter proprieties in East Jersey is a matter of record; it would seem his aforementioned brother-in-law had dropped his lawsuit by then. But Sonmans was still, apparently, broke—because of difficulties arising out of King William's War, he claimed—and this, on top of his evidently vindictive personality and his alliance with antiproprietary leaders Dockwra and Saltar, likely explains his hostility toward Woodbridge. After all, following another flare-up of animosities between the legislature's pro- and antiproprietary factions, the 1706 New Jersey Assembly broke up in protest over the Blind Tax debacle (despite Governor Cornbury's proclamation demanding that the assembly meet), and the House of Representatives not only tried Bowne on April 30, 1707—with Pike and Dennis as witnesses—but also expelled and imprisoned Bowne for refusing to return the money he'd collected.

Interestingly, Elisha Parker—one of Woodbridge's representatives to the House and printer James Parker's grandfather—was the only dissenting vote in Bowne's trial. Meanwhile, Governor Cornbury denied any connection to the scheme, and his backroom involvement only became apparent much later, when it was examined by historians like Weeks. Indeed, following Bowne's trial, so many antiproprietary heads had rolled that the only real blowback Woodbridge's freeholders experienced was the continued annoyance Sonmans created by preventing the town from establishing its boundary with Perth Amboy.

Of course, as minor as this issue might seem today, it was very important locally at the time. So, as the lawsuit against Sonmans lagged, Woodbridge continued its attempts to establish a boundary, appointing a committee on May 3, 1714, to run a line between the two towns. This attempt, too, came to naught, even further agitating the freeholders, and it is reasonable to suspect that at least part of their anxiety was due to how Woodbridge kept ending up on the proverbial hook for the sizable legal fees requested by its successive representatives in the case. (For example, on October 20, 1710, the town had to sell twenty acres of common land to pay its attorneys.) The larger issue, though, was that Woodbridge's freeholders owed quitrents for whatever land lay within the town's boundaries but couldn't use or tax a piece of land if it was considered part of Perth Amboy. Thus, the situation got so bad that the freeholders even offered to buy Sonmans's proprietary rights to obviate further costs.

Meanwhile, as for Sonmans, although his initial motive for gumming up the Woodbridge–Perth Amboy boundary may have been to exact revenge against Pike and Dennis, it also probably occurred to him that there were practical reasons to muddy the waters. After all, by claiming Woodbridge owed a quitrent on land that Perth Amboy taxed and also paid a quitrent on, he was essentially double-dipping as a proprietor.

Perhaps, then, this is how the name Stelle wound up alongside Sonmans's in the New Jersey Supreme Court's final decision on the matter. Gabriel Stelle was another prominent resident of the Amboys who, in 1728, founded a ferry service that ran between the Amboys before heading on to Staten Island. His name, coincidentally, first appears in Woodbridge's records of the case on March 24, 1727. Presumably, then, Stelle was the freeholder on Sonmans's Perth Amboy proprietary holding, and this is presumably how he got roped into the whole mess. At any rate, during the March 24, 1727, town meeting, John Kinsey Jr. was appointed the attorney for yet another investigative committee—consisting of Adam Hude, John Kinsey Sr., Benjamin Force, Daniel Britton, William Bunn, James Thomson, Shobel Smith and Moses Rolph—whose first task (decided during the December 15, 1727, meeting), was to directly discuss the boundary issue with Sonmans. This committee was ineffectual, and yet another committee—consisting of John Vail, Captain Matthew Moore and Rolph—was formed on January 9, 1730.

Also worth noting at this juncture is that, by this time, John Pike evidently was no longer involved in the Sonmans-Stelle case, and those who did get involved could find themselves targets of Sonmans's machinations if they weren't wary. For instance, a decade after serving on the 1730 committee, Vail was evicted, between 1741 and 1742, by the "Elizabethtown Associates" based on the invalidation of a deed Sonmans had sold him even as Vail had been working on the Sonmans-Stelle case in April 1732. Evidently, Sonmans wasn't above granting deeds of questionable validity to those who challenged his proprietary authority. If this unfortunate outcome is any indication, the freeholders were risking their livelihoods and wealth in taking on the conniving Dutchman. And yet, as the records also show, they never wavered in their pursuit of the case, with each regularly contributing ten shillings when called upon to pay Woodbridge's attorneys. Then, on

February 5, 1730, they also agreed to a plan, drawn up by attorney John Kinsey Jr., to lease the land in question to John Kinsey Sr., who would hold it in trust and have use of the timber on it for seven years—after which time the lease would automatically renew unless the town paid Kinsey a shilling to quit the property. The plan also mentioned that if the town paid Kinsey the one-shilling fee, he could re-enter the property, at which time Gabriel Stelle could also re-enter it and, in the presence of witnesses, escort Kinsey off the premises, thus recommencing the court case.

This arrangement apparently worked for a while, since the Sonmans-Stelle case doesn't reappear in the town annals until 1734, when, at the February 4 meeting, Kinsey and Rolph were replaced as the town's attorneys by Ezekiel Bloomfield and Shobal Smith. Then, as with most factual stories, the long troublesome affair over the boundary with Perth Amboy abruptly ends. The following month, Sonmans died, effectively leaving the matter up to his son, Peter Sonmans Jr., who doesn't seem to have inherited his father's vindictiveness: at the April 1 meeting, a penultimate tax of seven shillings was levied against every Woodbridge freeholder to pay Bloomfield and Smith, and in May, presumably feeling confident about their chances in the case, the freeholders voted to lay out the contested land into lots for the town's seventh and final division and to assess a final tax of fourteen shillings each for the last of their legal expenses.

Yet, Bloomfield and Smith may have had to reimburse the freeholders. For, when the case at last went before the colonial supreme court the following year, Peter Sonmans Jr. and his attorneys didn't show up, handing the ruling to Woodbridge by default. After this, in 1737, the younger Sonmans and his brokers, Samuel and John Nevill, offered to purchase the land from Woodbridge—an offer the town happily accepted. At the time, Kinsey's plan for leasing the land in trust was in effect, with Henry Freeman as the lessee, so there were no squabbles over the town's decision to sell. Better still, in exchange for a "clear and perfect title" to the 120 acres on the Woodbridge side of the now fully instated Woodbridge–Perth Amboy boundary, the younger Sonmans agreed to give the town three and a quarter proprietary shares, thereby defraying Woodbridge's past, present and future tax burdens with the portion of quitrents that would be due to the town as a proprietor in itself.

Thus it was that Woodbridge's freeholders ended up fully owning their town and freeing themselves from quitrents for the next half-century (when the American Revolution finally put an end to proprietorships). After almost three decades of continuous legal wrangling, the town was finally free of the Sonmans case. The outcome was better than anyone could have imagined when, in 1709, John Pike first filed suit: the boundary line between Woodbridge and Perth Amboy that still exists today was at last permanently fixed, and what's more, the town's antiproprietary freeholders—both those whose forefathers had fallen victim to the Nicolls grants and those who hadn't—finally had what they'd long desired: self-taxation. To celebrate, the freeholders voted on May 17, 1737, to sell additional land recovered from Gabriel Stelle on the third Tuesday in June 1737 to pay the remainder of their legal fees—and to split any remaining funds from the sale among themselves.

CHAPTER III

START A REVOLUTION

Woodbridge in the Era of Discontent

After establishing their town as New Jersey's quintessential crossroads and freeing themselves of proprietary quitrents, the people of Woodbridge began the second half of the eighteenth century with a hopeful outlook. Everywhere in the quickly expanding town, new homes, shops and businesses were springing up. And, with improvements to the overland postal system implemented after Benjamin Franklin became colonial joint postmaster general in 1753, culture, communication and the enjoyment of imported luxuries exploded. In short, the town was doing well, and perhaps no personal narrative captures the spirit of the era better than James Parker's.

Strolling along Rahway Avenue near where it meets Main Street today, you might notice a squat, green-shingled building with red and white trim and what always seems like a fresh coat of paint. This is Woodbridge's modern reproduction of the Parker Press, the first permanent printing press in New Jersey. It was founded between 1751 and 1753 by prominent Woodbridge native James Parker, who was born in 1714 to Samuel Parker, the son of founding settler Elisha Parker.

As a young man, James Parker learned his business well, apprenticing under New York's first printer, William Bradford, whose *New York Gazette* Parker helped publish from 1725 until sometime in May 1733. Then, at age nineteen, Parker broke his apprenticeship to Bradford by running away. Such an escape was a serious matter, as it constituted a breach of contract. Indeed, records show Bradford did advertise for Parker's capture and return

The green building on Rahway Avenue isn't James Parker's original printing house—which Tories burned during the Revolution—but a reproduction built to commemorate the U.S. bicentennial. *Michael Provance.*

on May 21, 1725. But it also wasn't uncommon for an apprentice to escape as he neared the expiration of his contract; as related in *The Autobiography of Benjamin Franklin,* the founding father himself broke his apprenticeship to his brother James at age seventeen and absconded to Philadelphia.

Even so, Parker was still a fugitive as a result of his escape and so dropped out of the historical record for nine years, presumably to avoid capture. During this time, Troeger and McEwen speculate he may have worked for his mentor and, later, business partner, Benjamin Franklin. Whatever Parker was doing, though, he doesn't resurface again until sometime between 1742 and 1743 to start his own publication in New York, the *Weekly Post Boy*, after Bradford had discontinued his *Gazette*. Each copy of the *Weekly Post Boy*, Dally tells us, was printed front and back on a single sheet of foolscap, or folio paper, which measured seventeen by thirteen and a half inches and was folded to create four pages measuring eight and a half by thirteen and a half inches, each about the dimensions of a sheet of legal-pad paper, or a broadside.

Aside from its significance as the first publication Parker put out himself, the implication of this endeavor could not be of greater personal importance, since it signaled Parker was no longer a wanted man. Apparently, Bradford had relinquished all claims against Parker by this time, or Parker certainly never would have been so bold as to publish a magazine under his own name. (While it was not uncommon for a former master to release an escaped apprentice from claims against a broken apprenticeship, it certainly wasn't expected.) So, based on this, as well as Parker's glowing tribute to his former master when Bradford died in 1752, we might easily conclude that the two had reconciled.

Within Woodbridge's reproduction of the James Parker printing house are all the accoutrements of an eighteenth-century printer, including an operational "screw" press. *Historical Society of New Jersey.*

In any event, the *Weekly Post Boy* proved a successful endeavor for Parker, for he continued publishing it even after his return to Woodbridge and added to his publishing schedule the *Independent Reflector* (from 1752 to 1753), the *New American Magazine* (from 1758 to 1760), and the *Constitutional Courant* (1765). According to Troeger and McEwen, while all three periodicals garnered attention and sold scads of issues, Parker was forced to discontinue two of them because of reactions to their politically charged content. Evidently, we must assume, Parker became something of a Whig as anti-British fervor swept through the colonies.

In the case of the *Independent Reflector*, which was edited by William Livingston, who later became New Jersey's first post-Revolution governor, some British subscribers were so angered by the opinions expressed in the publication's pages that they threatened to not only pull their subscriptions but to have Parker's lucrative government contracts—as New Jersey's provincial printer—cancelled. At issue, as Gordon Bond points out, was commentary featured in the *Reflector* by several prominent New York attorneys over whether King's College (now Columbia University) would be an Anglican or secular school. The lawyers took up the anti-Anglican side of the argument—a definite no-no in a time when the Church of England held so much sway, and this resulted in Parker's magazine ending its run even as it broke new ground for the power of the press.

As for the *Constitutional Courant*, although it was New Jersey's first newspaper, it so vehemently denounced Parliament's recent Stamp Act that Parker was nearly accused of sedition for it and had to discontinue it after just one issue. Troeger and McEwen suggest it was perhaps Parker's then-journeyman and former apprentice William Goddard who published it, but the fact that Parker, as postmaster, distributed it to other cities, including New York and Boston, indicates otherwise. Further, the fact that it bore the first reprinting of the "Join or Die" snake since that image's original use in the 1754 publication of the Albany Plan may even imply a connection to Benjamin Franklin. The truth is that no one really knows whether the *Courant* was intended as a one-off manifesto or who was responsible for writing and typesetting its contents, because reaction to it led to its immediate suppression and because it was printed pseudonymously under the attribution "Printed by Andrew Marvel, at the Sign of the Bribe refused on Constitution-Hill, North-America."

So, although he never got his own nose dirty, per se, Parker is at least tangentially tied to two of the Era of Discontent's most incendiary publications in the lead-up to the American Revolution. But this isn't to say that he was only a proto-muckraker; he also published magazines and newspapers intended to be serious business ventures. For instance, his *New American Magazine*, published while Parker was partners with William Weyman (between 1753 and 1759) and edited by Perth Amboy's own Samuel Neville under the pen name "Sylvanus Americanus," seems to have had a relatively decent run for the period by offering "a variety of entertaining and instructive matter" in each forty-page issue. While his business partner John Holt continued running the day-to-day operations of his New York press, in 1755, Parker also established, on behalf of Benjamin Franklin, a press in New Haven expressly for the purpose of publishing Connecticut's first newspaper, the *Connecticut Gazette*.

Moreover, Parker also, notably, published several of the first books printed in New Jersey, including the second volume of *Nevill's Compilation of the Laws of New Jersey* in 1761 and *Conductor Generalis*, a guide for New Jersey's justices of the peace, in 1764. Even more important to local history buffs was his 1765 publication, in Burlington, of the first history of the soon-to-be state: Samuel Smith's 574-page *History of New Jersey*.

Still, the most lucrative jobs for Parker were his public contracts, including his stint as New York's postmaster and as comptroller and secretary of the

This rack of printing-die trays in Woodbridge's reproduction of the James Parker printing house bears witness to how much publishing technology has evolved over three centuries. *Historical Society of New Jersey.*

postal department for the Northern District of the British Colonies—no small position, in fact, since (again, much like Franklin) it likely allowed Parker to lower postage rates for his own publications and raise them for his competitors'. What's more, he was called upon time and again to serve as New Jersey's official provincial printer under order to produce whatever paper materials the government needed, including lottery tickets, records of legislative proceedings and paper money.

For example, when Parliament refused to issue additional paper currency in 1764, perhaps concerned that doing so would inflate the pound sterling, New Jersey found itself quite literally hard up for cash. Indeed, there had never been much money in the British colonies because, as Gordon Bond points out, London had intentionally kept the colonies on barter economies to ensure their subservience and productivity as sources of raw materials. Among the many commodities traded in the colonies, then, corn was made legal tender in Massachusetts in 1631, and tobacco was officially recognized as such in Virginia in 1642, while wampum—the official currency of New York as late as 1701—was commonly traded to Native Americans in the northern colonies in exchange for beaver pelts. As for New Jersey, specifically, the initial barter goods of choice were the peas and wheat in which Governor Philip Carteret originally required quitrents be paid. In fact, Woodbridge's first freeholders, on at least one occasion, purchased twelve pounds of gunpowder from one Samuel Edsall with three thousand barrel staves, frequently paid their ministers in foodstuffs and, when the two wolf pits they had constructed in 1671 failed to protect the town, set a series of increasingly higher bounties on wolves to be paid by the town's constable in pickled pork—arguably the origin of the phrase "pork-barrel spending."

By Parker's time, though, New Jersey had had enough of peas, wheat and pork; already, in 1690, Massachusetts had started the trend of abandoning the barter system when it issued fiat (i.e., backed only by the public faith) "Bills of Credit" to help fund a military expedition into New France during King William's War. Afterward, several other colonies followed suit, including New Jersey in 1710. So, when the colony found itself short from financing its part of the defense against Pontiac's Rebellion in 1763 and Parliament refused to circulate more bills, New Jersey's government commissioned Parker to print more cash.

Of the two main concerns in printing paper money during the period, the matter of inflation was the easiest to deal with, as the commissioned printer was to print only the exact number of bills the government requested. Indeed, according to Bond, New Jersey was better than many other colonies at stemming the inflationary effects of fiat currency, and its secret was that it never set the number of bills it requested higher than the amount of currency it expected to collect in taxes the following year.

What the colony wasn't so good at curtailing, however, was the second major concern—forgery. As a matter of fact, this is still a concern among governments today. But, before the advent of magnetic strips, elaborate watermarks and a single national currency, it was exceptionally difficult to keep counterfeiters from simply replicating a fiat bill in bulk, thereby crashing the currency's value. Therefore, Parker's first concern in printing a new run of New Jersey bills was to discourage counterfeiting at all costs. To this end, the top of his design features—in large, bold letters—the reminder, "To counterfeit this Bill is DEATH."

Furthermore, the bills—printed in such denominations as one shilling, six shillings, thirty shillings and six New Jersey pounds—also featured intricate, difficult-to-replicate frameworks and the impression of an actual tobacco leaf, not only because tobacco was the most valuable barter good in the early colonies but because, like fingerprints, no two leaf impressions were the same. Thus, having personally handed over his proofs to colonial authorities and destroyed the original leaf, Parker could rest assured that if anyone tried to replicate his bills, he wouldn't be on the hook for a death sentence. Not only could a counterfeiter be caught through the government's comparing its proofs against potential forgeries, but those same authorities would know that Parker knew the true bills couldn't be replicated, having insured himself against it in their presence.

But, as Bond also explains, this isn't to say that Parker didn't have run-ins with the law over forgery accusations. The printer's repeated oaths to never counterfeit and the many notices of discovered counterfeits he'd published in the *Post Boy* notwithstanding, in 1770, Parker's press was fingered for

Thirty Shillings.

To counterfeit this Bill is DEATH.

Woodbridge, in New-Jersey.

+ Printed by James Parker. +

Shown here is a thirty-shilling colonial bill of credit printed by James Parker for New Jersey's colonial government; notice the tobacco-leaf imprint intended to prevent forgery. *Public domain.*

counterfeiting by one of the Woodbridge printer's former journeymen, Lewis Jones.

All this came about because Jones had attended the theater one night in New York City with a fraudulent ticket, and upon his being caught, authorities discovered a whole cache of similar tickets. Because Jones and Parker had parted company on bad terms, Jones said Parker's son, Samuel Franklin Parker, gave him the bogus tickets. In response, though, Parker pointed out that Jones's accusation was impossible, because though Samuel did work at his father's shop, the younger Parker was travelling in London at the time. Even more damning for Jones, Parker opened the doors of his shop to investigators to show them why the fake tickets couldn't have come from him: on the tickets were imprints of flowers unlike anything in his shop. Besides, the question of motivation must have come into play, for it's hard to imagine a successful businessman of fifty-three scalping phony theater tickets while sending his son abroad on vacation.

This satisfied authorities that Parker's hands were clean, and upon their subsequently discovering the flowers in question and their imprints on the genuine tickets printed in the shop of Jones's employer—another of Parker's former journeymen, Hugh Gaine—the proverbial jig was up. Jones immediately confessed to having forged the tickets and subsequently, it seems, was set free with a slap on the wrist.

The matter would have ended there, except that, not long after, we find Parker writing his old friend Benjamin Franklin to say, "About three weeks ago, [Jones] was apprehended and taken up for Uttering Counterfeit Jersey Bills. What the Evidence is I know not, but tis said several Bills he had passed away is returned on him, and I was told, that Saturday last, three Bills of Indictment were found against him on which he has been arraigned, and this Afternoon I hear he is to have his Trial, and [then] it's generally thought he will be convicted, and I know of no Instance of that Sort in this Colony ever being pardoned."

The subtext here, of course, is that if Jones were convicted, he would hang. So, even as he suffered from gout, Parker's paternal dread for the young man was almost palpable. In yet another letter to Franklin on April 24, 1770, he wrote,

Last Night Lewis Jones was tried on two of the Indictments…about 9 o'clock at Night, his Friends came to me, pleading for me to assist him with a Character [witness], *&c. I had not been out of my Room for 8 Days, and I could scarcely crawl. I went, and the Court indulged him by Waiting till I came. I related how he came to this Country, and spoke all I could in his Favour, and the Judge gave as favourable a Charge as a Man could do, on which the Jury acquitted him, on those two Indictments; but there is still another to come on this Day, which I hear has a more unfavourable Aspect.…I have done all I can, out of Regard for his Parents, who I know must pungently feel the Grief it must occasion them.…He never was any Advantage to me, but as my Son informed me,* [Jone's] *Father was particularly kind to him in London. I should be ungrateful if I did not do my Possibles in Favour of his unhappy Son; and wish my Ability was such as would enable me to do more.*

Obviously, at the time he wrote the main body of the above letter, Parker was all nerves, while Jones undoubtedly spent the night pacing his chilly, cramped cell. For both men, the thought of the noose tightening around young Jones's neck must have been suffocating. It seems Parker must have drowsed as he wrote, reclined as he probably was due to his condition, for at the very bottom of the page appears the simple postscript, "Lewis is acquitted."

The following day, Bond reports, Parker again wrote to Franklin to inform him that the newly freed Jones had paid a visit to thank Parker for his help and that "He [Jones] entreated I [Parker] would not write the News to his Father—he promises Amendment of Life so I submit to you not to acquaint his Friends with it. He may thank your Name for the Judge's favourable opinion of him." Then, Parker adds, "I contributed as much as I could, towards getting [Jones] a Passage to So. Carolina, where he will get Employ, and if he behaves well think he may retrieve some of his bad Fortune."

So, the matter of Jones's forgeries was settled once and for all with, as Bond points out, Parker dropping Franklin's name to the judge. Yet questions remain as to why Parker would have presumed to detail the story to his wealthy and esteemed friend and why dropping Franklin's name would have mattered to the judge if Jones were merely one of Parker's former journeymen. Then again, the answers to these questions might lie in the date of Parker's writing, for on April 24, 1770, Franklin was in London attempting to persuade Parliament to lift the Townsend Acts of 1767. This is clearly evidenced by a letter Franklin wrote to his wife in Philadelphia the very same week (on April 20, to be exact) and explains why Parker was writing to the founding father in the first place; suffice it to say, if Franklin had been back in the colonies, he would have, presumably, heard about Jones's dire circumstances and could have dropped his own name in court if it mattered to him. What's more, we know Franklin had sired at least one illegitimate son, New Jersey's then-governor William Franklin, so why not Jones, too? At the very least, this would explain all the pointed references Parker makes to Jones's "father" and the kindness shown to his own son in London.

Or maybe this is all just the fancy of a historian looking for something to write about. Parker, we know, was widely applauded for his generosity and energetic involvement in local affairs; even as he resumed running his New York press with Samuel at the expiration of former partner John Holt's lease in 1766, he also acted as a lay reader and officiant for Trinity Episcopal Church and served as a township justice of the peace and captain of an area "Troop of Horse." Considering how much Parker was involved in civic life, then, it would be no surprise for him to have a sheerly humanitarian concern for Jones's wellbeing. It's also little wonder that the poor printer died in 1770 at only fifty-six, just a few months after he'd saved the wayward Jones. Officially, his cause of death was gout, but anyone looking at the facts of the matter would probably agree that he'd worked himself to death.

In any event, soon after James Parker's death, Samuel Parker rented out the printing shop in New York and sold the press in Woodbridge only to see it burned by several Tories during the British occupation of Woodbridge. He did, however, have his father interred in the Kirk Green of the elder Parker's beloved Woodbridge, and James Parker's monument still stands there among his peers' russet shale headstones surrounding the Old White Church. His press, meanwhile, was resurrected when the present-day replica was constructed in 1974—not just in honor of the national bicentennial but as a fitting tribute to one of the town's most beloved native sons.

WARS AND RUMORS OF WARS:
THE REVOLUTION COMES TO WOODBRIDGE

During the American Revolution, the entirety of New Jersey was a major military theater—and for good reason: it bordered two of the colonies' largest ports, New York City and Philadelphia, and most of the major north-south highways ran through it, including the colonial precursor to the Turnpike, the King's Highway. Thus, from a strategic perspective, the British effort to capture New Jersey was a practical matter; if they succeeded, they would effectively cut the rebellion in half, strangling the colonies' ability to provide material support to each other and to receive supplies from allied France.

Suffice it to say, then, Woodbridge was soon embroiled with the rest of New Jersey in the chaos that ensued as war broke out. According to Dally, Loyalist "Tories were treated as strangers by those who hitherto had lived near them as neighbors," and the freeholders cancelled all further town meetings after March 12, 1776, as residents gathered in the Elm Tree and Cross Key taverns and nervously listened over rum or cider to travelers' accounts of the latest news from Boston. Among those in Woodbridge most interested in developments were likely Charles Jackson, owner of the Elm Tree Tavern (which once stood along what is now Rahway Avenue across from the Barron Arts Center and was named for the massive elm in its front yard); town clerk Robert Fitz Randolph Jr. and his brother Nathaniel "Natty" Fitz Randolph; justice of the peace Ebenezer Foster; Samuel Franklin Parker (James Parker's son); Dr. Moses Bloomfield; Reverend Azel Roe; Nathaniel Heard; Robert Clarkson; John Shotwell; Benjamin Thornell; James Ayers; Samuel Jaquish; Isaac Freeman; William Moore Jr.; James Bonny; James Mundy and William Smith. These men, all of them known Whigs, helped organize and participated in the actions of the Woodbridge chapter of New Jersey's Committee of Correspondence after the town closed its port to British imports and exports. What's more, many of them also participated in the war effort itself.

Probably the most prominent among them, though, was Heard, who was commissioned a colonel of a battalion of militiamen on February 12, 1776. The militiamen in question were naturally a subdivision of the 1st New Jersey Regiment, the famous Jersey Blues—so called, as Troeger and McEwen tell us, for their distinctive uniforms, which, during the Revolution, consisted of blue-black tricorn beaver hats and scarlet-lined, royal-blue jackets with gilt-pewter buttons over red vests; in other words, they were exactly the picture most modern Americans have of Revolutionary War soldiers.

Of course, the reason New Jersey's original "boys in blue" entered the popular imagination is that they saw more action during the Revolution than nearly every other American unit. As New Jersey's original fighting force, they first formed in Piscataway in 1674, all the way back when Governor Carteret first ordered Piscataway, Woodbridge and Perth Amboy to organize a militia to repel raids by Native American tribes allied to the Dutch. Under Heard, the unit first saw action against the British as early as February 1776, when the Continental Congress ordered the colonel and his five hundred blues to raid the Long Island Tory towns of Jamaica, Hempstead, Jericho and Oyster Bay and to capture a Loyalist munitions store. According to Dally, during these raids, Heard's men sang "Yankee Doodle" and even invented their own verse:

> *Colonel Heard has come to town*
> *in all his pride and glory,*
> *and when he dies, he'll go to hell*
> *for robbing from the Tories.*

The cultural import of this initial raid aside, it was the first in a string of engagements for Heard's men. Subsequently, on June 17, 1776, New Jersey Provincial Congress president Samuel Tucker ordered Heard and sixty of his men to capture Loyalist New Jersey governor William Franklin—founding father Benjamin Franklin's son—in Perth Amboy. Some historians claim Heard captured Franklin on the front steps of the Proprietary House, while others assert they captured him in bed. Of these, Dally's account—that Franklin wasn't keen on waking that night to find the blues in his bedroom—is probably the most colorful. Whatever the case, though, the governor refused to give his parole (his promise as a gentleman that he would henceforth stay out of matters as a prisoner of the Continental Army), so he was shipped off to Princeton for trial, then to Connecticut, where he remained in the custody of Whig governor John Trumbull for the next twenty-eight months. Later, he was exchanged for a patriot prisoner, giving him the chance to assist British supreme commander William Howe in New York, but, sadly, he never saw his wife, Elizabeth Downes Franklin, again, for she died in New York a year after his capture.

As for Heard, he and his men occupied the Amboy barracks following Franklin's capture as part of a one thousand–man force encamped in Woodbridge, Blazing Star and Perth Amboy. This was a necessity for the revolutionaries, since Staten Island was a Tory stronghold, making the

Son of founding father Benjamin Franklin, Governor William Franklin served as New Jersey's last colonial governor from 1763 to 1776, when General Heard captured him. *Public domain.*

rumors that it would serve as a launching point for a British attack that August a serious threat. To prevent an invasion, Commanding Brigadier General Heard (he wouldn't be a fully commissioned brigadier general until February 1, 1777) was reinforced in July 1776 by the 2nd Pennsylvania Battalion and by 450 Middlesex Jersey Blues under Major Duychink. For the most part, the 2nd Pennsylvania merely marched through Woodbridge on its way to reinforcing Perth Amboy, leaving only one company of 100 men under one Captain Wilcox to guard the town. Meanwhile, Duychink's Jersey Blues initially deployed to the seaside slopes of what is now Sewaren.

Yet, perhaps because of the Americans' preparedness, the rumored attack never came, and Heard ordered Duychink's men to Perth Amboy on July 6. There, based on General Washington's orders, he had them settle in as a policing force to arrest any Loyalists undermining the patriot cause, while the 2nd Pennsylvania moved north to assist in Washington's defense of New York City. They were followed, in August, by the rest of Heard's men, as part of the 3,300 troops Washington requested as reinforcements on June

14. It was then, while serving under General Nathaniel Greene at the battles of Bedford Road and Brooklyn, that Heard—who had only recently (on June 25) been promoted to commanding brigadier general—was placed in command of the sixteen companies (comprising 160 officers and 1,762 enlisted men) encamped at the Kingsbridge area of the Bronx. This force, hereafter known as "Heard's Brigade," would assist in the evacuation of New York on September 12.

AFTER WASHINGTON'S RETREAT TO Philadelphia, Woodbridge's only defenders were a handful of native Jersey Blues who'd stayed behind, leaving the town's other residents to take action themselves. For example, Reverend Azel Roe, who'd begun preaching ever fierer sermons against the British as the war progressed, called on his parishioners to join him in attacking a British unit at Blazing Star. Considering the bulk of this makeshift force must have consisted of old men like Roe himself, certainly, the British easily prevailed. In fact, Roe ended up a prisoner and was shipped off to the infamous Sugar House Prison, a dilapidated warehouse in lower Manhattan near where the Brooklyn Bridge now stands. But, according to legend, the irascible, rotund reverend didn't go peacefully: when the officer in charge of marching him to Manhattan offered to carry the minister across a small ford on their route, Roe mounted his corpulent mass on the poor man's back, remarking, "Well, sir, you can say after this that you were once priest-ridden."

Similarly, a little later, a group of British soldiers—presumably the same men who had skirmished with Roe—requisitioned 400 head of cattle and 200 sheep from the townspeople to feed themselves through the winter but were foiled by a unit of Middlesex Jersey Blues in the early morning of December 11, 1776. This was probably the same incident Dally connects to resident Ford Cutter, a Jersey Blue born in 1757 who would eventually be severely injured at the Battle of Monmouth. What is certain is that the Blues recovered every last animal, but how they did so is another matter altogther, for 600 animals wasn't a haul they could have easily snuck away with. According to Dally, Cutter heroically crept into the redcoats' pen on Strawberry Hill and, finding his own oxen among those corralled there, led every last creature from captivity when his own beasts followed him out. Of course, Dally has a tendency to indulge his imagination, but that doesn't mean Cutter wasn't part of a successful cattle raid all the same.

Moreover, while we can't be exactly sure *how* the Woodbridge blues managed to get back the town's cattle, we know where they met beforehand: at Timothy Bloomfield's house at Fords Corner. At the very start of the war, Bloomfield, an avowed Whig, had been too old to serve, but he hadn't been too old to open his home on New Brunswick Avenue and King Georges Road to anyone willing to give the British a licking. As a result, it wasn't long before several Tories kidnapped him and marched him to the infamous Jersey Prison Ship—a squalid, cramped coffin of a vessel for more than 11,000 Americans. Worse still, the Loyalists hanged Bloomfield at least twice, to the point that he lost consciousness, for refusing to swear allegiance to George III. Yet, obstinate even in the face of death, the moment the old patriot revived, he reportedly spit in his tormentors' faces and denounced the king more vehemently. Indeed, according to Dally, Bloomfield was so outspoken that it was only for fear of his extended family (which included the Dunhams and Fitz Randolphs) that his captors didn't kill him outright.

As for what happened in Woodbridge during Bloomfield's captivity, with his sons Smith and Timothy Jr. both in the militia, his wife, Sarah (née Ford), and daughters, Eunice and Sarah, were left vulnerable to British and Tory looting. Dally records that, because among the Bloomfield men were two revolutionary soldiers and a Whig instigator, the redcoats targeted the Bloomfields' farmhouse for one raid after another and, during one, carted off the family's Bible and their brindle cow, Bossy.

Immediately following the theft, poor Eunice and another girl—probably her sister, Sarah—trekked from Fords Corner to the docks on the Arthur Kill, hoping to hire a ferry so they could attempt to recover their holy book. Suffice it to say, this wasn't the safest of journeys at the time, especially for one or more daughters of a Continental sympathizer. Somehow, though, the two made it, only to find, once there, that no ferrymen had half the moxie they did, so there was no one to carry them to Staten Island.

Well, resourceful gal that she was, Eunice pulled an abandoned scow into the water, and the two girls paddled themselves across. Having reached Staten Island, they were then, according to Dally, courteously escorted by one redcoat sentry agape at having watched their brazen voyage. Before long, they were standing in front of the British commander—likely Tory colonel Christopher Billop, whose Bentley Manor estate sat on the island's southern tip. Naturally, the girls wasted no time making their case for the family Bible. They likely plied Billop's ear with a litany of the depredations they'd suffered since the war had carried their brothers and father away. Whatever was said, though, the colonel apparently became so gushy from their tale that he directly sent for the book and asked if they'd lost anything else in the raid. At this, we can almost imagine the plucky Eunice responding, "Well, sir, there is the matter of our cow."

Again, there are no records of the dialogue, but the effect of Eunice's words was that the British commander personally accompanied the girls to the pasture where his forces were grazing several purloined heifers. Upon seeing Eunice, old Bossy supposedly trotted right up to the girl and began nuzzling her, providing all the proof Billop needed to release the animal to the fresh-faced young maiden of nineteen. Then, he ordered his men to escort the girls, Bible and cow back across the Arthur Kill in what we must assume was a much larger craft than the one in which the girls had arrived.

Following so much kindness, we might imagine the Bloomfield women were tempted to view the British in a new light. But come that evening—or sometime afterward, at any rate—any reconciliatory mood Billop's kindness might have inspired was surely spoiled when someone opened the family Bible: in it, some Tory fink had scribbled obscenities about Smith Bloomfield beside the young soldier's birthdate entry. After this, we may surmise, the Bloomfield ladies decided to keep up Timothy Sr.'s practices, and their home continued as a meeting point for patriots with even the most harebrained of attack plans.

For instance, one night in July 1776, just before Washington's retreat from New York, the Bloomfield house hosted a meeting of several boys too young to join the militia. These boys, having heard that a British warship was docked at Perth Amboy, had apparently decided to lug Woodbridge's old swivel cannon, "Old Sow," south to fire on the ship. After some preliminary commiseration, then, the unnamed urchins (and possibly the Bloomfield gals themselves) somehow managed to pull off their prank, carting Old Sow to Perth Amboy with a team of oxen and planting the cannon in the churchyard of St. Peter's Episcopal Church. From these heights overlooking the docks, according to Dally, they fired a single, fist-sized ball at the British brig as the moon rose over the harbor at eleven o'clock. Then, they scattered down Rector Street to hide as the ship returned fire from one of its full-sized guns, the immense cannonball crashing through several of the graveyard's headstones, including that of one Gertrude Hay, whose memorial still bears the marks of the British bombardment.

Well, certainly, the aforementioned boys were out of their depth, and it would be little surprise to learn that one or two of them wound up dead. But, quite the contrary, besides the obvious property damage, the stunt resulted in minimal consequences: the British, ostensibly spooked by the possibility that General Heard's brigade had returned from the major fighting in Brooklyn, turned tail and set sail. So, these Woodbridge pranksters were left to celebrate their defeat of an entire enemy warship thanks to firing a single piece of ammunition the size of a softball.

Even as Woodbridge's women, children and elderly pulled together to defend their homes, by the spring of 1777, the tide of the war in New Jersey was turning in favor of the Continentals. The first hint of this came on January 6, when a unit of Jersey Blues recovered 1,000 bushels of salt after a two-hour skirmish saw the British so thoroughly licked that they had to call in reinforcements. Then, on February 1, 1777, 1,000 British, armed with three heavy guns, engaged 700 Americans outside Piscataway, and as it so happened, the Americans killed 36 British soldiers, forcing the redcoats to fall back until their reinforcements arrived with three additional cannon. What's more, on February 23, 1777, Brigadier General William Maxwell's 2nd New Jersey Regiment dealt heavy losses to the 3rd British Brigade, killing as many as 500 men when the redcoats detoured through Spanktown on their way to New Brunswick to capture Maxwell. And, on March 8, 1777, Maxwell again showed the British what for when his 2nd New Jersey forced an expeditionary unit led by General Howe to retreat at "Spunk" (or Punk) Hill near Bonhamtown.

Thus, despite several comparable American losses—such as General Adam Stephen's loss of twenty-seven men to the 71st Scottish Regiment (or "Royal Highlanders") on May 10, 1777—the Americans' string of small successes convinced Howe to abandon New Brunswick on June 22, 1777, and move the bulk of his forces to Perth Amboy. From there, on the evening of June 25, he and General Charles Cornwallis undertook a make-or-break attempt to capture General Washington himself, who, an American defector had notified them, had led his forces out of the Watchung Mountains after being holed up there for several weeks. The initial British plan was simple: Cornwallis's column of 8,000 men would cross the Arthur Kill from Staten Island and meet up with Howe's 9,000 men at Perth Amboy. Then, Howe would lead 12,000 men west through Metuchen, while Cornwallis marched

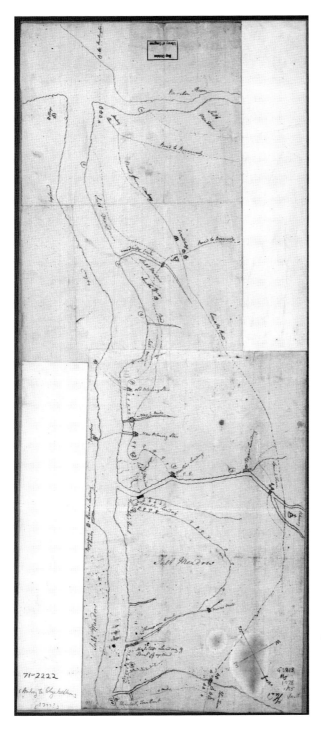

This Revolutionary-era map showing the Jersey coastline during the Battle of the Short Hills may be British because it's oriented southward, from a New York perspective. *Library of Congress.*

the remaining 5,000 and their fifteen cannon up what is now Amboy Avenue into Woodbridge and, turning right at today's Green Street, follow Oak Tree Road all the way to where it converged with Howe's route. There, the two columns would recombine before again splitting to flank the Continentals near Quibbletown, with the ultimate objective of surrounding Washington's 7,000- to 10,000-man army (accounts vary) at Plainfield.

Well, to paraphrase a poem Scotsman Robert Burns penned nine years later, the best laid plans of mice and men often go awry: the morning after Cornwallis's column landed on June 26, 1777, the British had marched a mere three miles before they were waylaid at 6:00 a.m. near Strawberry Hill by a 150-man detachment of Colonel Daniel Morgan's Rangers under Captain James Dark. This was the start of the portion of the Battle of the Short Hills that would come to be known as the Battle of Ash Swamp, or the Oak Tree Engagement. According to Dally, it began after sixteen-year-old militia scout Robert Coddington—later a local Revolutionary hero in his own right—led Dark's men to the farm of Daniel Moore, where some British light horsemen and footmen were having breakfast. Troeger and McEwen claim the scout was thirteen-year-old Jonathan Freeman, but whoever first spotted the British, as Dally points out, their lavish uniforms must have seemed both terrible and awe-inspiring in the morning sun:

No doubt there was great hilarity among the red-coated soldiers as they partook of the rustic dinner [sic]. *We imagine we see them scattered in picturesque groups over the wide field, with the blue smoke from many campfires rising in languid spiral columns from the ashes and embers. There pace the vigilant sentinels; here dozes a sleepy teamster; there prance the cavalry horses; here gleams the burnished steel of a stack of muskets; there flutters the bunting of England—the British cross; here reclines a thoughtful officer in the brilliant uniform of the Royal Light Horse; there is a busy aide de-camp hurrying from company to company; here is a noisy crowd discussing the probable issue of the campaign. In graceful attitude stands not far away the bugler with his highly polished cornet in hand awaiting the word of command. When the clear ringing notes are heard at length the aspect of the whole camp is changed. The men vault lightly into their saddles, the drums tremble with the rapid strokes of the loud "call to arms," the infantry fall into line; and, as if by magic, the hour of uproar and feasting is succeeded by the complete silence of human voices. The birds sing gaily in adjacent woods, save which only the heavy tread of splendid troops is heard as they move to the tap of the drum.*

A volley is heard. There is a halt. A man here and another there fall wounded in the ranks. There is a hurried consultation. When the smoke clears away a body of American infantry is descried, opposing the further advance of the invaders.

To be sure, there is no actual historical support for this description beyond the hearsay Dally gathered in the 1870s from Robert Coddington's son, Robert Jr. But what *is* known is that, upon spotting the Americans, four of Cornwallis's battalions quickly broke off their breakfast, formed ranks and positioned themselves and their six heavy cannon on the high ground, while, as per Mayers, 250 British riflemen returned fire with new breech-loaded rifles invented by their commanding officer, Captain Patrick Ferguson. The new guns loaded faster than the standard muzzle-loaded guns of the period, letting Ferguson's men fire up to six shots per minute. And, even sadder, many of the British soldiers rolled their ammunition in verdigris prior to loading their guns. Thus, their shots poisoned and killed many Americans whose injuries would have otherwise proved little more than flesh wounds.

Despite this deadlier, superior firepower, though, the skirmish held up Cornwallis's entire column for nearly a half an hour before a massed bayonet charge forced Dark's men to flee up Oak Tree Road. In response, the British did what any army would do under such circumstances and gave chase. What Cornwallis didn't know, however, was the number of soldiers Washington had dispatched to the area under Major General William "Lord Stirling" Alexander to protect the Continental army's northern flank. In fact, Stirling commanded a 1,798-man force comprising detachments of divisions under Brigadier Generals William Maxwell and Thomas Conway, as well as 700 of Morgan's Rangers and four New Jersey regiments under Colonels Israel Shreve, Matthias Ogden, Elias Dayton and Ephraim Martin. By the time Dark's men broke, then, Stirling had already deployed Conway's Brigade as well as an unnumbered force of Jersey Blues, about 700 Pennsylvania German Volunteers (known as "Ottendorf's Corps") and three new French brass cannons to support the rangers.

Consequently, Dark's remaining men joined ranks with the Pennsylvanians under General Maxwell and French colonel Armand-Tuffin as their British pursuers closed in, and at about 8:30 a.m., the boom of the French ordnance, secreted along the tree-lined roadway, was heard as the front ranks of the pursuing British fell where they stood. This was near where Plainfield and New Dover roads intersect with Oak Tree Road, and Mayers records that fighting during this portion of the battle devolved into hand-to-hand combat, causing one unit of Pennsylvanians to lose thirty-two out of eighty men. Presumably, then, the initial cannonfire must have been at nearly point-blank range, and British losses must have been commensurately staggering. In any event, though, Cornwallis seems not to have recognized that Stirling was using the same tactics the French and their native allies had used against Washington and General Braddock a quarter-century earlier during the French and Indian War. So, when Ottendorf's Corps fell back to Woodland Avenue and New Dover Road, the redcoats again gave chase.

Eventually, having saved their cannons, the Pennsylvanians retreated to Martin's Woods, about a mile closer to the Short Hills, and Cornwallis's first column—consisting of, in addition to cavalry, four regiments of grenadiers (three Hessian and one British), one unit of Hessian Chasseurs (a light-infantry unit), and one unit of the Queen's Rangers—continued on along Oak Tree Road. Then, at the intersection of Old Raritan and Inman Roads, the British again met resistance from the 1,000-man New Jersey Brigade, which Lord Stirling had deployed in a defensive line along Rahway Avenue and Tingey Lane, near the Short Hills Tavern. Upon sighting the Brits, the dug-in Americans once more fired cannons stashed behind trees and brush on the high ground, cutting down Cornwallis's vanguard as it advanced toward the eastern side of the Short Hills.

Meanwhile, Hessian lieutenant colonel Von Minningerode's Grenadier battalion attacked from Inman Avenue. They tried encircling Lord Stirling's position by heading north around Ash Swamp (on the site of today's Plainfield Country Club), hoping to prevent his escape to Westfield as thousands of Cornwallis's muskets and his fifteen cannon opened fire on the American line. Amid continual blasts of grapeshot from Stirling's four French three-pounders, the British fixed bayonets and charged, and subsequently breaking through the American defenses alone, with all of his men apparently wounded or dead on the field behind him, British captain John Finch rushed one of Stirling's cannons and chased away its crew with nothing more than a pistol. Then, as per Mayers, Finch turned and, spotting General Alexander himself, blustered, "Come here you damned rebel and I will do for you"—to which Stirling responded by ordering four nearby sharpshooters to mow down the man.

And yet, with wave after wave of bright-crimson jackets continually, stolidly marching across the field toward Stirling's position, the battle's outcome was inevitable: over the course of two hours, Stirling's cannon were lost and retaken several times before Cornwallis's men finally took all but one (saved by French colonel Armand) and the Americans again fled. Mayers claims that Lord Stirling's horse was shot out from under him and that General Maxwell was nearly captured by Von Minningerode's Grenadiers. However, Dally paints a different picture of Stirling's retreat—one gathered from local lore that explains why the battle would go down as a disaster for the British.

Even Mayers admits that Von Minningerode's men, in their attempt to encircle the Americans, were surprised in Ash Swamp by the remainder of the Pennsylvania Germans, who immediately fired a cannon full of grapeshot at the Hessians, killing six with the first shot alone. But Daily's account goes on to explain how this was yet another of Stirling's ambushes—and the deadliest yet. Not only did the confrontation between the Pennsylvanians and Hessians see the two sets of Germans screaming at each other in their shared Teutonic tongue as bayonets and musket balls shredded their bones and flesh; Dally asserts that Cornwallis's British Light Horse, chasing what they presumed was another unit of routed Americans, also plunged into Ash Swamp. It was at this point, Dally says, that their quarry—having rejoined the remaining Pennsylvanians fresh off repelling the Hessians—turned and fired from behind the swamp's gnarled tree trunks.

As we might imagine, by the time the British realized their mistake, it was too late. Dally claims their horses slid and sank in the mire as the patriots slowly, surely surrounded their enemies, each taking a shot before doggedly trudging through the morass to his next cover. Reloading and firing, reloading and firing, the Americans, in Dally's account, found their marks again and again as the British horsemen, slick with mud and gore, struggled to stand or crawl from beneath their lifeless mounts. Some escaped, of course. But, on the whole, in Dally's account, Cornwallis's Light Horse was soon just a jumble of dying men and beasts.

If true, the resulting panic among the cavalrymen would have been complete and the regiment literally decimated. In fact, Dally claims the carnage was such that every nearby home was filled with the cries of the dying that night and that, the next morning, local boy Noe Clarkson had to use oxen to pull a sled of water for those left in the field as sappers worked to inter stacks of bodies in a pit dug in one of the Clarksons' fields. Further, many local residents, primarily women and children, were just returning home in the wake of Cornwallis's advancing British force when they were confronted with the horrific piles of mud-splattered corpses. One resident, Ezra Mundy, would later recall to Dally that, as a child during the battle, his mother had taken him and his siblings to a dilapidated barn near the local schoolhouse as the ill-fated British Light Horse regiment passed. Apparently, several other families of revolutionary soldiers had also taken refuge in the same barn, and at one point during the fighting, a stray cannonball crashed through one of the barn's walls. Miraculously, none of the occupants were hit. Rather, we might imagine the smell of the freshly dead swelling in the morning sun the next day left such an impression on Mundy that he could recall the experience in detail nearly a century later.

Meanwhile, according to Dally, General Howe's numbers showed Stirling's men only killed five British, wounded thirty others and captured thirteen prisoners, while Howe also recorded an American loss of sixty-three killed and more than two hundred wounded and captured. And yet, we have to cast an askance glance at these figures—not only because Lord Stirling's numbers contradict them, but because if they'd been accurate, the British would have probably achieved their objective. Rather, what's likely is that Washington deployed Lord Stirling's forces for the express purpose of harrying Cornwallis while the rest of the Continental army escaped back into the Watchung Mountains. Moreover, the commander in chief probably never meant to engage the combined might of Howe and Cornwallis but was merely baiting them, and Stirling's brief, blistering ambushes around Woodbridge were part of that plan; by the time the militiamen retreated at Metuchen, they had already stalled Cornwallis's column enough to stymie its joining Howe's. That Stirling's retreat also allowed him to avoid the onslaught that would have ensued had Howe's column reinforced Cornwallis's was just tactical expediency.

So, when the recombined British force finally did near the main Continental force, it was already depleted enough to dissuade Howe and Cornwallis from their planned assault when they were confronted with an additional strategic reversal: Washington had removed the bulk of his troops from the lowlands at Quibbletown to the mountains around Westfield. From here, America's first commander in chief could see and fire ordnance on every British movement in the plains below, making the original plan to flank Washington impossible and making any assault on the Continentals' position an assured bloodbath for the British.

Indeed, Washington's redeployment was such a game changer that the Watchung Mountains are still called "Washington's Rock." And so, the British generals took the only option left to them: they reformed their columns about-face and beat a retreat back down the long, bloody road to Perth Amboy, suffering a second round of guerilla attacks when Scott's Light Horse and Morgan's rangers flanked their rear. They camped in Rahway before resuming their retreat, and this only gave the Yankees another chance to form ambushes along the remainder of the route. As a result, British losses over two days of marching were so severe that Howe and Cornwallis removed the bulk of their forces from the Amboys on the last day of June 1777, thus ending Britain's occupation of the Woodbridge area.

FOLLOWING HOWE AND CORNWALLIS'S defeat at what became known as the Battle of the Short Hills, Tory residents of Woodbridge found the tables turned against them. Incidents of Whigs tarring and feathering Tories and vandalizing their properties and possessions became frequent, and many Loyalists abandoned the town for Staten Island in the wake of the British retreat. In response, the Whig faction seized the Tories' land and auctioned it off, but this didn't prevent citizen justice from precipitating something of a witch hunt; even the mere suspicion of being a Tory spy was enough to get a person lynched, so some of those who fled may not have actually been working with the British but may have instead simply been social outcasts. One anecdote recorded by Dally, for instance, concerns a suspected Tory spy living near the town docks: apparently, once the town had forbidden crossing the Arthur Kill, this man became aware that his neighbors suspected him of spying, and consequently, he became so desperate to escape that he hauled off a huge trough used by the neighborhood cider mill to catch crushed apples. He then supposedly dragged the unwieldy thing to the shore and rowed to Staten Island by cover of night, using a shovel—which he'd also purloined from the mill—as a paddle.

To combat anti-Tory vigilantism, New Jersey instituted the New Jersey Council of Safety, which, on August 16, 1777, ordered a detachment of Major Reuben Potter's company under Colonel Frederick Frelinghuysen to escort the wives and minor children of fled Tories (including John Heard, Ellis Barron, William Smith, Isaac Freeman and Samuel Moores) across the Arthur Kill to Staten Island under a flag of truce. However, this gesture of human decency apparently went unnoticed among the Loyalists, as their raids continued throughout the remainder of the war. For instance, on January 30, 1780, it was so cold, according to Dally, that the Arthur Kill froze, creating a walkable route between Staten Island and Sewaren that thirteen Tories rode across to kidnap nine revolutionary soldiers and several young ladies they were escorting at Rahway.

Nevertheless, perhaps those who suffered most during the war were Woodbridge's Quaker residents, for their commitment to pacifism brought reprisals from both Continental and British authorities. For instance, at the sect's November 1778 monthly meeting, member William Thorne resigned his appointment to a war-relief committee to be replaced by Edward Moore because, he said, he was being forced, by threat of imprisonment, to confirm his allegiance to the Continental Congress. Indeed, the animosity displayed during the Revolution toward noncombatants, who were frequently seen as Tories, made accepting imprisonment much harder for the Quakers than in previous conflicts. Gone were the days of compassionately setting a Friend free on a flimsy excuse; instead, Quakers like Marmaduke Hunt were marched to the Morristown jail, confined in what Hunt described as a "Nausious" [*sic*] cell, and "deprived of the Necessaries of life to that degree that [he] could procure no more for [his] support but one meal for seven days." As a result, Friends like Hunt and John Laing reported swearing allegiance to the United States in fits of "unwatchfulness."

However, the greatest threat to Woodbridge's Quakers was undeniably the fact that so many of their young men joined the fight. Perhaps one of the most famous of these former Quakers—for their signing up always precipitated their permanent ejection from meetings—was Nathaniel "Natty" Fitz Randolph, whose family must have left the sect when he was a boy as part of the Fitz Randolphs who disavowed Quakerism after another Nathaniel Fitz Randolph caused a stir in 1759. According to Dally, the older Nathaniel's ejection occurred because he had alleged two other prominent Friends had said things to offend him, and when it was shown that they hadn't, and the Nathaniel in question still refused to retract his accusations, the Woodbridge Quakers disowned him at their monthly meeting in 1762. As a result, the Fitz Randolph clan was split, with some, like the immediate family of Woodbridge's Natty and Robert, quitting their connection to the Society of Friends. This, in turn, ensured that the name Fitz Randolph would become inseparable from

The Nathaniel Fitz Randolph named in the dedication of this relief at Princeton University's Nassau Hall should *not* be confused with Woodbridge's heroic "Natty" Fitz Randolph. *Djkeddie.*

any discussion of Woodbridge during the Revolution, for Natty would became one of the town's greatest war heroes.

Apparently, Natty, Robert and several other Fitz Randolphs who fought became involved after the American victory at the Battle of the Short Hills had cleared the immediate vicinity of redcoats, and they probably first mustered in late 1777 as Generals Maxwell and Heard assembled two thousand militiamen at Elizabeth to drive the British out of Bergen County at Hackensack. In fact, although no evidence of this exists, it isn't altogether unlikely that Natty was one of the new militiamen recruited for this October campaign, since there is no previous mention of him. If so, the British had their many raids on the Woodbridge area to blame for convincing him to sign up.

As for Natty personally, according to Dally, he was a "character" to his fellow Woodbridge residents. "Active and intelligent," he is described as the exact opposite of his brother Ezekiel, who is said to have regularly passed out while making deliveries on his butcher's cart. In contrast, Natty quickly rose to captain of the Middlesex Militia and is said to have refused a colonel's commission to remain with his men—although he would later accept an honorary appointment as naval officer for the Eastern District of New Jersey on December 12, 1778, at which point the revolutionary council presented him with a sword in honor of his "patriotism, vigilance, and bravery during the war."

All these honors were due to the many heroic attacks he had already made on the British that same year. The first, for instance, involved him and just fourteen others attacking the enemy on Staten Island the night of Wednesday, June 24, 1778: according to a Loyalist account recorded by Dally, Natty's unit rowed across Newark Bay from Elizabeth and surprised and wounded two British guards before racing back to their boat with the enemy tailing them. But, as Dally also suggests, this was likely the raid during which Natty and his men captured several British soldiers, because around the same time, Washington exchanged letters with the governor regarding some prisoners Natty had taken. It might also be the same raid on Staten Island during which it's said Fitz Randolph and his men came across a group of Hessians, one of whom shot Natty in the left arm. As this legend has it, the injury only irked Natty, and he motioned to the German soldier who'd shot him as if he wanted to share a secret. Then, when his would-be assassin was close enough, Natty grabbed the Hessian and slung him over his right shoulder, carrying him away as a prisoner in front of the German's stunned comrades.

Similarly, another time, it is said, Natty was alone when he came across a British baggage train traveling between encampments. Knowing no fear, the American waited until nightfall before leaping from his hiding place, brandishing his sword and shouting, "Come on, boys! Here they are! We've got 'em!" Well, supposedly, the wagon drivers were so shocked that they jumped from their seats and ran without a second thought—leaving Natty with their vehicles, which he commandeered for himself and his men.

However, subsequent to this and similar acts of derring-do, the revolutionaries and their civilian supporters gave Natty the nickname "tower of strength," and he started bragging that the enemy would never take him alive. Well, the British reaction to this was exactly what you'd expect: they began trying to capture him, and on at least two occasions, they temporarily succeeded.

During the first of these occasions, according to Dally, Natty had snuck home to visit his parents in Woodbridge when three mounted, armed Loyalists began pounding on the Fitz Randolphs' door. Apparently, as his mother, Mary Fitz Randolph (née Shotwell), then informed Natty, the men had been creeping around the house all day and, on hearing them announce themselves, she moaned, "Why *did* you come home, Natty? You know the Tories are determined to take you!"

Despite what we can only imagine was an "Oh, now you tell me" moment for Natty, his mother's worries that the Loyalists would lock him up in one of their prison ships or Sugar House, and his inability to count how many Tories actually awaited him outside, the captain was unruffled. He supposedly snatched his sword and pistols from the shelf where he'd laid them, then flung open the front door, loaded gun drawn, and shouted, "*I* am Natty Fitz Randolph, and no three men can take Natty alive. The first who tries is a dead man!"

The oft-recounted story then claims that, in response, the three terrified Loyalists immediately dropped their weapons and allowed Natty to march them away at gunpoint until they reached the edge of the neighborhood, at which point the trio made a break for it and, mounting their horses, galloped back toward Staten Island.

Likewise, the second time the British succeeded in capturing Natty, they had cornered him and his men. But, according to Dally as well as Troeger and McEwen, the militiamen continued fighting until the only one left standing was Fitz Randolph himself. Of course, Natty had taken his share of knocks, having been hit several times so that blood streamed down his arms, legs and flanks. Yet, the captain still continued fighting, brazenly bowling over the redcoats ringing him with nothing more than the butt of his musket. This supposedly went on for several minutes, because the redcoats' officer, admiring Natty's badger-like tenacity, had commanded his men to take Fitz Randolph alive. Eventually, though, the officer was forced to beg for Natty's surrender so his troops wouldn't have to kill such a brave enemy. With musket still raised, as Dally tells us, Natty stopped swinging at the widening ring of British and, after a moment's consideration, agreed—but only if the officer promised him good treatment and an early exchange. The officer having so promised, then, Natty finally dropped his gun and allowed the Brits to bind his wrists. As per his pledge, the officer reportedly ensured Natty's relative comfort in jail, and the captain was exchanged soon thereafter. According to Dally, the British officer would later claim Natty was the bravest man he'd ever met.

Finally, there was a third British attempt to capture Natty, and this one stuck. It occurred sometime in January 1779, when Fitz Randolph was again leading a scouting party on Staten Island. This time, Loyalists under one Captain Ryerson pursued Natty and his men across the island. According to the story, Natty ducked into a house to evade his pursuers, but Ryerson's men didn't have the decency of Natty's previous would-be captors and instead laid low until Captain Fitz Randolph had set down his sword and gun and settled in for the night. Then, the Tories sprang on the house, presumably kicking in the door and grabbing Natty before he could reach his weapons. They also, presumably, had to bind the captain in some way, since it's hard to imagine the heroic Natty going peacefully. Whatever the details, the facts are that the incident ended with the Tories hauling Fitz Randolph away to one of their prisons in New York City, where he would remain, enduring both neglect and torture, until May 26, 1780.

As Natty rotted in a prison, other Woodbridge natives took up the fight, including Captain James Heard, one of General Nathaniel Heard's sons and a member of "Lee's Legion" starting in 1779, as well as Robert Coddington, a fifer in the Middlesex Militia and the Continental army, and Henry Freeman, a fifer in Captain Asher Fitz Randolph's company of Jersey regulars. There was also David Coddington, Robert's brother, and Peter Latourette, as well as several men Woodbridge contributed to Sheldon's

Light Dragoons, including Captain John Heard (another of General Heard's sons), Jeremiah Clarkson, Jeremiah Dally, Joseph Gilman, Jonathan Jaquish, Jedediah Freeman, Lewis Dunham and Captains David Edgar and James Paton, who were not only brothers in arms but brothers-in-law.

Probably the most exciting incident in which any of these men were involved was the capture of Colonel Billop in a 1779 raid so daring it was once wrongly ascribed to Natty—though, since he was in prison at the time, Natty couldn't have been involved. The ringleader of the raid was, in fact, David Coddington, as Dally relates, and among the four or five men who joined him were his brother Robert and Peter Latourette. The story goes that the men, all members of the local militia, had been watching Billop's mansion on the southern tip of Staten Island for some time from the steeple of St. Peter's Episcopal Church in Perth Amboy. This was apparently a favorite lookout point for the Americans and British alike, as the church stands at the very edge of the heights overlooking Perth Amboy's harbor; in a time before the russet glow of billions of lightbulbs dominated the area's night sky, you could easily see a gnat sneeze on Staten Island from the church's bell tower. Thus, on June 23, 1779, when they spotted the colonel taking an after-dinner stroll about his lavish grounds, the militiamen quickly boarded what we can only guess was probably a dinghy, and under cover of darkness (during what Dally insists was an extraordinarily dark night), they rowed with muffled oars across the Arthur Kill to Ward's Point.

Quickly putting ashore, they then stole up the beach and onto the estate single file, and giving a drowsing guard a password they'd received from an unnamed African American woman—perhaps one of Billop's slaves, considering the period—the men managed to sneak into the colonel's bedroom and abscond with the snoozing Tory before anyone else in Bentley Manor was the wiser. The only casualty of the entire affair was apparently Billop's horse, which was shot after one of the Americans tried to steal it, and the poor animal refused to get into the militiamen's boat. This shot was the first indication Billop's men had that anything was amiss, as the revolutionaries had, up to that point, been careful to avoid alarming the enemy, gagging and restraining the colonel for good measure. As a result, Coddington and his men were practically back in Perth Amboy before the redcoats managed to muster a rescue expedition. Nor does it seem the British pursued the matter, insomuch as the militiamen were able to deliver Billop to the Burlington jail the following November with nary another mention of the incident recorded.

Whether this story, related by Dally, is historical fact or local lore is unknown. But, to be sure, Billop's capture did happen and was a major win for the Woodbridge militia not only because of Billop's rank but because he was a homegrown Tory officer. Whigs and Tories, you see, were far more vicious with each other than with the professional soldiers Britain trucked in from Europe. Thus, the colonel's Whig captors decidedly did *not* roll out the red carpet for him despite his rank and importance to General Howe's command; rather, they treated Billop worse than any common private they held in Burlington during the same period. In retaliation for the ill treatment they'd heard comrades like Reverend Roe, Timothy Bloomfield and Natty Fitz Randolph were receiving at Sugar House and elsewhere, they fed the colonel a scant ration of bread and water. And, in response to a complaint received from the Tory colonel, the prison commissary replied as follows:

Elizabethtown, Nov. 6, 1779
Sir:

Sorry am I that I have been put under the disagreeable necessity of a treatment towards your person that will prove so irksome to you; but retaliation is directed, and it will, I most sincerely hope, be in your power to relieve yourself from the situation by writing to New York to procure the relaxation of the sufferings of John Leshier and Captain Nathaniel [Fitz Randolph]. *It seems nothing short of retaliation will teach Britons to act like men of humanity.*

I am, sir, your most obedient servant.

~Elisha Boudinot

Of all the surviving notes passed during the period, this is one of the funniest for its signature Jersey sarcasm. But, clearly, the colonel's treatment was no laughing matter to the Americans. They had, after all, already learned of the thousands of men who had died in British detainment, and the prisoners Boudinot mentions above weren't the only members of the Woodbridge community to suffer this outrageous fate. For instance, Jonathan Inslee, a longtime Whig—as well as the Coddington boys' grandfather—had fallen into Loyalist hands when they first swept the town for radicals following Washington's retreat into Pennsylvania.

The Tories who'd captured him had been particularly sadistic, forcing the sixty-one-year-old man to wade through a river on his way to prison, then refusing him dry clothes upon their arrival in New Brunswick. As a result, though his wife, Grace (née Moore), had dutifully followed her husband on foot and successfully obtained his immediate release, the poor old man died soon thereafter on February 24, 1777. This, of course, explains the extreme hatred the Coddington boys harbored for the British. In fact, it is actually surprising that Billop didn't receive worse treatment at their hands. Even so, the colonel ostensibly remained in good health—despite his spartan diet—until his exchange on December 26, 1779.

As for the others mentioned in the list of local heroes, perhaps the next-most important personality, after Captain Fitz Randolph and the Coddingtons, was Peter Latourette. You see, when Latourette learned that one British Captain Jones was laid up with a cold in the old, stone tavern at Port Richmond, Staten Island, he and his fellow Jersey Blues saw their chance to free their beloved Natty. Knowing a sick man would be easy to carry off, the six-foot-two Latourette and three or four of his comrades—the Coddingtons probably among them—resolved to nab the British officer to use in an exchange.

Thus, dressed as civilians, the militiamen crossed Arthur Kill in broad daylight and found themselves entirely ignored by the handful of guards posted outside the Staten Island watering hole. According to Dally, the redcoats weren't the slightest bit suspicious when the New Jerseyans began scuffling in the barroom. Instead, the Brits thought the brawl was the evening's entertainment. They egged it on and began horsing around themselves—to the point that they distractedly set down their guns before sitting down to dinner in the next room. This was when, having heard the coughs of the ailing Captain Jones, Latourette and his men sprang into action: they absconded with the guards' guns and burst into the officer's room, gagging the British captain with his snot rag to keep him from alerting his guards. Then, they carried Jones to their boat and crossed the Kill Van Kull to Bergen Point, where they kept the British officer in the Bergen jail until they could exchange him for Natty.

And so, once more free, Natty, like any hero, went straight back to fighting, and within three weeks, he and his men were among those firing on the British retreat through Middlesex County in the last and bloodiest battles in New Jersey—the Battle of Connecticut Farms and the Battle of Springfield.

Unlike the Battle of the Short Hills, these battles didn't occur on Woodbridge soil, but one part of the British force did land somewhere near Woodbridge from a launch point on Staten Island. Then, on June 6, 1780, this group joined another unit camped near Elizabeth and marched northwest toward Morristown. Their objective was to capture General Maxwell's brigade then sweep south toward the Watchung Mountains, where Washington was still keeping the bulk of his forces. Washington had presumably caught wind of their plan, however, because he ordered every revolutionary unit he could muster to occupy the Short Hills. Subsequently, when the British showed up near Connecticut Farms on June 7, 1780, they were repulsed and retreated in a merciless rainstorm toward Perth Amboy—only to be dogged over the next day by American militiamen firing from behind fences, trees, stones and every other sort of cover available.

British losses during this series of guerilla skirmishes were high, but so, too, was the number of Americans killed. Washington *had*, after all, called in every militiaman and regular unit in the neighboring towns, including the men of Woodbridge. Among those from Woodbridge involved in the fighting were Jeremiah Clarkson; Jeremiah Dally and his father, Samuel; a man named Brown; Captain Paton; and Smith Bloomfield, as well as the whole kit and caboodle of Natty's boys.

Sadly, Natty himself was also among those killed, having been hit in a particularly vicious firefight at the Battle of Springfield on June 23, 1780. Subsequently, he died of his injuries (or so tradition holds) exactly one month later, on July 23, 1780, and was buried in Kirk Green around the Old White Church. Otherwise, the exact particulars of Natty's death were not recorded, though we might imagine that if Natty fell, no one fighting in his vicinity survived to tell the tale, either.

As for the Woodbridge dragoons, meanwhile, Captain Paton also suffered a major injury on June 8, 1780, during the fighting at Connecticut Farms, and he somehow—miraculously—recovered. At the time, he had been temporarily acting as an officer in Captain Obadiah Meeker's "Essex Horse" under Lord Stirling. And, though, as with Natty, the particulars of Paton's wounds aren't recorded, he apparently acted so heroically that Major William Crane, present at the battle as commander of the 1ˢᵗ Battalion of Essex Militia, wrote of him, "He behaved with spirit and bravery through the whole course of the alarm till wounded and taken."

Still, the captain himself remained ever humble. For instance, in his June 30, 1780, letter to Captain Edgar, who was still in Connecticut enlisting dragoons, he focuses less on how he'd received his wounds and more on his recovery:

Dear Edgar:

I am happy to be able to once more write to an old friend, which is more than I expected so soon. Must inform you that on Tuesday, the 6th inst., at night, the British army landed at the Point and marched near Springfield. On Wednesday [they] *burned all the houses and* [the] *Church in Connecticut Farms, and in the evening retreated in heavy rain to the Point. On Thursday all day was skirmishing, and unfortunately, dear Edgar,* [I] *received a very bad wound. The ball entered below my left temple and came out nearly opposite. I got it near the New Point and kept my horse until I rode to my uncle's house, when I dismounted, hitched my horse and walked in and was dressed and declared not mortal, but expected to lose the sight of my right eye. However, thank God, my eye has come to remarkably. I am able to walk in the garden. The wound heals very well. It discharges mostly out of my nose. I am in hopes it will leave little or no mark in my face. I was kept concealed in my uncle's house until the 19th, when I was made a prisoner and got a parole to return when called for. I never was visited by a doctor during eleven days. Miss Aggie dressed me all the time.*

I am not able to give you the particulars of the expedition, only [that] the brave Captain Nathl. Fitz Randolph was wounded the last day the British troops marched to and burned all of Springfield, and is since dead and much lamented. Smith Bloomfield is also mortally wounded and not expected to live, I believe. It is impossible to describe the distress that prevails in this part of the world. My heart aches with writing; you must excuse me. I believe all friends are well. My uncle, aunt and Miss Aggie join in compliments, and believe me to be, dear Edgar, your sincere friend.

~James Paton

Despite the apparent gruesomeness of his wounds, Paton survived the Revolution and lived for another quarter-century. After the war, he received a 1788 commission from Governor Livingston to captain of the 1st Battalion of Middlesex Militia and, in 1792, a commission from Governor Paterson to command the early Light United States Cavalry. He then served on Governor Bloomfield's staff in 1811, holding the rank of lieutenant colonel, from which he was promoted to major and given command of the 1st Regiment of Middlesex Militia. Indeed, he would live to age fifty-eight, surviving his first wife, Captain Edgar's sister Hannah, by fifteen years and Captain Edgar by five years before dying on November 6, 1816. The two fast friends and comrades in arms are buried near each other in the churchyard of the First Presbyterian Church, not far from Natty Fitz Randolph.

⟫⟫⟫⟪⟪⟪

As WE ALL KNOW, the American Revolution would end with Cornwallis's capitulation at Yorktown, Virginia, three years after the fiercest fighting in New Jersey had ended, and the result, of course, was American independence. The only noteworthy incident left to tell of Woodbridge's involvement, then, is how the town celebrated one of its first Independence Days with a tradition still with us today every time a resident plants an American flag on her porch or in her yard: according to Troeger and McEwen, Jennet (or Janet) Gage, aunt of the illustrious Zebulon M. Pike, became "the Molly Pitcher of Woodbridge" when she erected the first liberty pole in town. She chose the pole, something like a modern flagstaff, from among the straightest, tallest hickories growing in the woods behind her house, bringing along her slave Joe and a yoke of oxen to fell and carry the burden to town.

In Jennet Gage's day, Woodbridge's Cross Keys Tavern was located at the intersection of Main Street and Amboy Avenue where the Knights of Columbus building now stands. *Michael Provance.*

Apparently, the irony of having an enslaved person do the hard labor of installing a "liberty pole" was lost on Gage, as it would have been on most others of her period. Nevertheless, this was how Woodbridge got its liberty pole, with Joe harvesting and trimming it, then loading it onto the cart. Then, the pair drove the pole to Jennet's home directly across from the Cross Keys Tavern—which now stands on the corner of today's St. James Street and E. Middlesex Avenue, just behind the 7-Eleven and across from American Auto on Amboy Avenue. There, they hoisted it erect, and Jennet raised the Stars and Stripes. Naturally, there is no record of whether Jennet used a rope and pulley to do so or simply nailed the flag to the top of the flagstaff before Joe set it in place. Either way, though, the effect was the same: after all the tribulations of the Revolution, including the seizure of Jennet's own home due to her husband being a Tory, Jennet's liberty pole seemed a fitting way to punctuate that bloody period.

CHAPTER IV

THE NEW REPUBLIC

The War of 1812 through the Progressive Era

I n the heady decades after the Revolution, Woodbridge flourished. Revolutionary army surgeon Dr. Moses Bloomfield's son General Joseph Bloomfield—himself a Revolutionary War veteran of the Battles of Brandywine and Monmouth—won New Jersey's fourth gubernatorial election in 1801 to become the state's sixth governor. He ran under Thomas Jefferson and James Madison's Democratic-Republican ticket (which would eventually evolve into the Democratic Party still with us today). And, though he would leave the state's highest office between 1802 and 1803 due to a tied election, starting after his 1803 win, he would continue as governor until 1812, becoming New Jersey's longest-serving governor before the twentieth century.

Elsewhere, Jennet Gage's nephew Zebulon M. Pike took part in America's westward expansion, leading an 1806 U.S. military expedition into the Louisiana Territory, which President Jefferson had recently purchased from France. Pike and his men made it as far as halfway up the highest mountain in the northern front range of the Rockies before descending what would become his namesake, Colorado's Pikes Peak, and being captured by the Spanish. He would then go on to serve in the War of 1812 until he was killed in action in Canada at Fort York (today's Toronto).

Other Woodbridge men who served in the oft-forgotten War of 1812 included, as per Colonel Malcolm B. Gilman via Troeger and McEwen, many descendants of local Lenni-Lenape, Piscataways and Rahwacs whose fathers and grandfathers had served in the Indian Scout Company during

Revolutionary War hero and Woodbridge native General Joseph Bloomfield served as New Jersey's governor from 1803 to 1812—the longest continuous governorship before the twentieth century. *Public domain.*

the Revolution and who enlisted in the Jersey Blues when the United States and Britain went to war a second time. However, at the war's end in 1814, these men found themselves caught up in questions of race that still torture the United States today. Assuming they had won their place in the community, many Native American veterans of 1812 had moved to town, attended Christian churches in Woodbridge and Piscataway and begun sending their

Possibly the oldest house on "Woodbridge's Park Avenue," 95 Green Street was built around 1840 by Gilbert Heard, son of General Nathaniel Heard's nephew John. *Historical Society of New Jersey.*

children to the Quaker free school in efforts to assimilate. Yet, in what can only be called a shameful blemish on Woodbridge's history, even as the town belatedly celebrated the war's end in February and March 1815—firing a cannon captured by the Coddingtons during the Revolution and mounting a parade, barbeque and gala attended by some three thousand residents—the Lenape veterans and their families were being rejected by the country and town for which they'd fought.

In 1820, for instance, the question arose in churches among white parishioners as to whether to bury their Lenape brethren in church graveyards, and some residents, like the Gilmans, resorted to burying their Lenape relatives in their family cemeteries at night to avoid public ridicule and, presumably, the bodies' disinterment. By 1840, then, Trenton forcibly removed many of the above-mentioned veterans' descendants, sending them to a 100,000-acre reservation in the Pine Barrens, then removing them again, on the eve of the Civil War, to a reservation in Western New York. Clearly, the message was that despite the Revolution's claims of equality, brotherhood and liberty, for much of the nineteenth century, these rights would only pertain to white, male residents of Woodbridge and beyond.

THE PECULIAR INSTITUTION: SLAVERY, QUAKERS AND ABOLITIONISM IN WOODBRIDGE

The problems Woodbridge's Lenape faced were hardly singular. As in every part of England's North American colonies, slavery had been practiced in early Woodbridge, and though it is impossible to determine who brought the first slaves into the town and when, by 1680, there were already 120 slaves in the entirety of New Jersey. Nor did New Jersey's white residents slacken in their demand for slaves, with the number of slaves reportedly rising from 3,071 in 1737 to 11,423 in 1790 and 12,422 in 1800—a population that comprised 5.8 percent of New Jersey's population at the time. Indeed, in 1810, there were 230 slaves permanently residing in Woodbridge alone. And these numbers don't account for the many people previously bought and sold in the town, for prior to the 1808 federal prohibition on importing slaves, the slave trade was an important sector of Woodbridge's economy, situated as it was on the Triangle of Trade's northwest corner. In fact, evidence documenting this hideous practice in the town comes down to us via Dally in the form of a June 3, 1717 receipt copied verbatim in his history:

> *Know all men by these presents that I, Shoball Smith, of Woodbridge, In ye County of Middsex In ye province New East Jersey, for and In consideration of ye sum of fifty pound Currant Silver money, of ye said province, to me In hand paid by Samuel Smith of ye same place, yeoman of ye town and province aforesaid—do bargain, sell, alienate and Deliver one Negro woman Named Phebe to said Samuel Smith, for him, his heirs and assigns.*

According to Dally, there is no sure evidence that Woodbridge had the sort of indoor marketplace early Perth Amboy had specifically for slave trading. And, insomuch as Perth Amboy and New York City were both important colonial slave ports where thousands were sold daily, it is unlikely Woodbridge was competitive in the industry. But we must also remember that on January 9, 1724, when the town's freeholders voted to make certain areas common land in perpetuity, such land was to be used for "marketplaces," as well as for schoolhouses, and that such marketplaces were seen as essential to any town's wellbeing in the period. Thus, the above receipt is likely the tip of the proverbial iceberg; though there is no evidence of an enclosed Woodbridge marketplace, the town certainly had an open-air market, and certainly

African American slaves were bought and sold there, with one tradition holding that this market sat on three acres at the corner of Green Street and Rahway Avenue where today's QuickChek and Walgreens now stand.

As for the victims of slavery in Woodbridge, little is known of their lives. Beyond the above receipt for Phebe and the role Jennet (or Janet) Gage's slave Joe played in raising the first liberty pole, the only other reminder that slaves existed in the town at all was an ornate slate headstone for a freed slave named Jack that long stood in the Presbyterian graveyard. Otherwise, what we know about slavery in Woodbridge is what we know of it throughout the northern colonies: it had existed to some lesser extent in Europe since time immemorial and was introduced to the town in the 1600s by both the Dutch and English; however, how the practice differed among the colonists from the way it had long worked in Europe was that England's colonies had legally codified "chattel" slavery, or the perpetual enslavement of individuals from birth to death and down through generations.

Moreover, what was stolen from slaves throughout British North America wasn't merely their labor; in that period, the sickening practice of slave "speculation" was all too common. Especially rampant after the United States banned the import of slaves in 1808, but widely practiced even before then, it involved male slaveholders purchasing slave girls as young as twelve and repeatedly raping them over their lifetimes, then selling the offspring of these unions—the slaveholders' own children—for a profit. In light of this, chattel slavery wasn't just a "peculiar institution," as the nineteenth century deemed it, but perhaps one of the most inhumane and disgusting practices in all of human history.

Of course, while slave ownership is a matter of public record, which Woodbridge residents practiced speculation remains unknown. What we do know, rather, is that without New Jersey's slave population and their stolen labor, Woodbridge and other towns would not have grown nearly as fast. It is for this reason that Britain's colonial governments encouraged the practice, with, for instance, colonial proprietors Sir George Carteret and John, Lord Berkley, granting freeholders extra land if they brought slaves to the colony.

It is little wonder, then, that, as historian Clement A. Price notes, "support for [slavery] was stronger in New Jersey than in any other northern colony," although New Jersey had the second-largest population of Quakers after Pennsylvania. And this support barely wavered in the wake of the Revolutionary War. We must remember, after all, that the war came just four years after the English Court of the King's Bench's ruled in 1772's *Somerset v. Stewart* that chattel slavery was inconsistent with British Common

Law—providing slave-owning colonists like Washington and Franklin an oft-overlooked additional impetus to revolt. Pennsylvania, in fact, was the only state to abolish the practice in the immediate wake of the Revolution, and it wasn't until 1804 that New Jersey's legislature passed its Act for the Gradual Emancipation of Slavery, under which every child born to an enslaved woman after the Fourth of July that year would be born free.

Yet, even this "gradual emancipation" had its dark side inasmuch as the children's mothers and fathers were to remain slaves, and children born as late as July 3, 1804, were legally compelled to work for their mothers' owners until they were twenty-one (if female) or twenty-five (if male). What's more, the act provided plenty of advance notice for the state's slaveholders to simply truck their pregnant slaves southward and sell them, thus making the freedom granted moot. Nor was there anything prohibiting wealthier owners from simply ensuring such children were born outside the state on family plantations in the South, thus legally perpetuating slave status. So, for those New Jersey slaves who weren't born *in* the state *on or after* July 4, 1804, the only hope for freedom, up to the passing of the Thirteenth Amendment on January 31, 1865, was still their owners' manumitting, or freeing, them.

Still, insomuch as it had always been too cold to grow cotton or tobacco in northern New Jersey, Woodbridge's nineteenth-century economy wasn't as heavily reliant on slavery as, say, Atlanta, Georgia's. And the number of slaves held in New Jersey steadily dwindled after 1804 to just 236 persons by 1850. Nor were all of Woodbridge's white residents entirely complicit in the practice, as its large Quaker population did regularly agitate for an end to it. Indeed, in the immediate aftermath of the Revolution, sentiments against the practice were so pronounced that, as Troeger and McEwen relate, Woodbridge's residents held an antislavery rally on the first Independence Day, July 4, 1783, at which non-Quaker Dr. Moses Bloomfield spoke on the inconsistencies of slavery and the ideals of the Revolution, then publically freed all 14 of his own slaves.

UNTIL NOW, WE'VE MOSTLY overlooked Woodbridge's Quakers, because though they were prominent before the Revolution, their story is most apropos to the town's relationship to slavery and its role in the Civil War. The first Woodbridge-area members of the sect arrived after the colony's split into East and West Jersey, about twenty years after the town's founding, and the first Quaker meeting at Perth Amboy was held on August 3, 1686, according to Dally, at prominent Friend John Barclay's home. Thereafter, the "Friends at Amboy" held meetings on what they called the "second fourth day of every month" (or second Wednesday), starting in the "ninth month" (November), and this continued until 1689, when their meetings moved to Woodbridge, where they purchased land for their meetinghouse on June 15, 1706, from former town minister John Allen. The Quaker meetinghouse stood where the United Methodist Church now stands on Main Street, and for those interested, Dally recounts in extraordinary—sometimes excruciating—detail the piecemeal process of the building's construction, as well as that of the sect's second meetinghouse in Plainfield, built in 1736.

However, what's really important about all these seemingly superfluous details is how quickly Quakerism expanded in Woodbridge. The reason for this had to do, in part, with neighboring West Jersey becoming a predominantly Quaker colony, but it also had to do with Woodbridge's charter-enshrined religious tolerance. Friends, after all, had been hanged, burned and imprisoned in Britain and New England. So, the fact that they enjoyed some support from East Jersey authorities is one reason Woodbridge became a haven for them.

It must also be remembered that Quakers, in attempting to reproduce the practices of early Christianity, did not, traditionally, have ministers, and as such, this lack of a hierarchy made determining what was and wasn't permissible among Friends a community matter hashed out in a democratic manner. Indeed, Woodbridge's Quakers seem to have debated every aspect of their lives, from whether to take down the headstones in their cemetery (in 1751) to whether it was all right for a man to marry his (presumably diseased) wife's first cousin (in 1755).

Among the Woodbridge Friends, at least, there were certain things every member could agree were not right: war, booze and slavery. On that last point, Woodbridge's Quakers were so vehemently opposed to the practice that when prominent Quaker John Keith advocated for "the emancipation of negroes after a reasonable term of service" (a progressive idea in its wider seventeenth-century context), at their June 17, 1738, monthly meeting, they censured every member who had purchased slaves. Of course, Keith was divested of all authority by the London Quakers in 1694, leading to his subsequent appearance in Woodbridge as an Episcopalian missionary. So, it's clear his "moderate stance" wasn't rejected by Woodbridge's hardline Friends alone.

Later, then, as per Troeger and McEwen, many Woodbridge-area Quakers would help fugitive slaves flee to freedom in Canada, feeding and hiding them as they arrived in town in the dead of night. In fact, of the twelve Underground Railroad routes that began at the northern shore of the Delaware River and crisscrossed New Jersey, the Number One Route ran straight through Woodbridge Township. There, "conductors" (often Quakers, freed slaves or other runaways) would help escapees avoid detection by the bounty hunters frequently patrolling the banks of the Raritan following the Fugitive Slave Act of 1850.

Still, this isn't to say that every Woodbridge Quaker's hands were clean. For instance, not long after their meetings permanently moved to Rahway and Plainfield, on the eve of the Revolution, arguments broke out among the Friends over the last slave "fit for freedom" still owned in their "jurisdiction." Presumably, by this they meant that one of their members still owned a slave, and it's likely this slave was Jonathan Harned's Mary, whom he delayed manumitting until shorty before his death in 1776.

So, in the end, while Quaker residents did lessen the popularity of slavery in Woodbridge—in contrast to what happened in neighboring towns like Perth Amboy and Newark—and most were never slaveholders, this isn't to say that all the sect's members were innocent. Ultimately, the question of whether some Americans should have the right to own others would prove impossible to answer peaceably in one small town or state. That answer could only come after the entire nation had paid a great cost—in both treasure and lives.

These Honored Dead:
Woodbridge and the Civil War

Driving home from work today, many Woodbridge residents often find themselves in bumper-to-bumper traffic along Main Street. Annoying as such standstills can be, what's fascinating is the everyday glimpse of history they offer—if you know where to look. Approaching the town's modern courthouse, for instance, with the sun finally vanished behind the green rail bridge in your rearview mirror, you're sure to spot the white pillar standing at the three-way juncture of Main Street, Berry Street and Rahway Avenue. This is Woodbridge's Soldiers and Sailors Monument, erected on December 1, 1911, by Thomas Jardin & Son to honor those who "[died] to

Erected in 1911, Woodbridge's Soldiers and Sailors monument—located at the three-way intersection of Berry Street, Main Street and Rahway Avenue—honors the town's Civil War dead. *Michael Provance.*

make men free," as Julia Ward Howe put it in the penultimate line of her "Battle Hymn of the Republic."

As contemporary journalist Michelle O'Rourke noted in an article on the monument for *The Corner*, "the soldier [who] has silently stood watch over Woodbridge for more than a hundred years" was funded through community drives, such as bake sales and tag days, over the course of five years and at a total cost of $3,000—the equivalent of around $80,000 today. The monument's three-point base, which makes the intersection such a hassle, actually represents the Third Corps of the Union army, to which many "Woodbridge Boys" belonged. The fact that the soldier on top is clutching a flag and facing southwest is in honor of John M. Sutton, after whom the sculpture is modeled, for saving his regiment's colors at both Gettysburg and Chancellorsville.

The monument's placement, meanwhile, is said to have been at Sutton's request, for the Civil War veteran supposedly refused all other honors and awards for his valor except the ability to view the town's monument from the porch of the Main Street grocery store where he worked. Also informing the monument's placement, though, was the location of First Lieutenant William Coddington Berry's childhood home, from which the ediface was also within eyeshot. Berry, you see, was the first of Woodbridge's casualties in the war, killed at Williamsburg, Virginia, on May 5, 1862. In fact, Berry's siblings helped spearhead the town's fundraisers for the monument by raising $2,100 through a certificate drive, thus determining where Sutton's likeness would sit long before the construction of Woodbridge's modern township building.

Of course, none of this was on the minds of Berry, Sutton or the fifty-one other Woodbridge Boys—such as future town postmaster Samuel Coddington—when they joined Company H of the 5th New Jersey Volunteers and Company F of the 28th New Jersey Volunteers. Presumably, after the Confederates fired on Fort Sumter in Charleston, South Carolina, on April 12, 1861, forcing President Abraham Lincoln to declare war, feelings were mixed. New Jersey was, after all, the only northern state to have voted against Lincoln in the previous election. Indeed, southern sympathizers in the town even hung an effigy of Lincoln from the Scudders School House liberty pole, which they'd greased in a perverse symbolic gesture that forced their enraged neighbors to chop down that symbol of '76 if they meant to save Lincoln.

Still, far be it from the descendants of those who'd fought at the Battles of the Short Hills, Connecticut Farms and Springfield to shy away from aiding their country in that dire hour: as per an 1861 order from Governor Charles Olden, members of Woodbridge's recently formed Pike Guard (including Berry, Sutton and Coddington) quickly combined with those of Rahway's Clark Guard to form Company H of the 5th New Jersey Volunteer Infantry, whose members signed on for three-year tours of duty. The 5th was then combined with the 6th, 7th and 8th New Jersey Volunteer Infantries into General Joseph "Fighting Joe" Hooker's division of the Union army's Third Corps. It's worth noting here that the Third would end up being one of only two Union corps to field just two divisions instead of three at Gettysburg due to the war's prior ravages.

Then again, we all know that old saying about hindsight; when the war started, the Woodbridge Boys in Company H were as gung-ho as anybody and so immediately started drilling in factory buildings owned by William H. Berry, father of the company's twenty-four-year-old lieutenant. The elder Berry had moved the family's hay-baling and -shipping business to Woodbridge from Jersey City in 1832 and, soon thereafter, opened a firebrick factory on Woodbridge Creek that produced one million bricks per year. It was, of course, unusual to drill in a factory. But, it comes down to us through Troeger and McEwen that the industrialist opened his facilities to Company H in the final few weeks before the soldiers headed south, perhaps intuiting it would be the last he'd see of his beloved boy.

As for Hooker's division, meanwhile, it is said to have been wild both on and off the battlefield, and consequently, the general's name is popularly associated with a common epithet for "ladies of the night." The truth is that the vulgar term is of a much older New York City–area coinage stemming from how the city's "houses of ill repute" once sat on "the Hook." Hooker's association with the word, then, may be attributable to the fact that so many of his men were from the region and enjoyed a good pun; certainly, we might imagine young Will Berry in camp, snickering along with Privates Sutton and Coddington at the general's unfortunate name after the bawdy houses of Washington, D.C., shuttered to prevent the spread of sexually-transmitted diseases among Hooker's men. If this association with "Hooker's girls" troubled the general, he didn't let on. Apparently, he remained as rambunctious as ever, as shown in the following anecdote, "Joe Hooker at the Poker Table," written within living memory of the war and published in the October 26, 1876, issue of *The Independent Hour*:

In 1862, President Lincoln said to General George Stoneman: "Stoneman, [I'm thinking] of giving the command of the Army of the Potomac to Joe Hooker. What do you think about it?"

"Hooker is a brave man," said Stoneman, "and has fine presence, but I have seen him in deliberate battle, and he did not impress me."

"Where?" asked Lincoln.

"At the poker table," said Stoneman. "You see [there], if anywhere, a man's whole character, his power to sustain defeat and loss, his adroitness, his ultimate strength or weakness. Now, Joe Hooker was fonder of cards than any man I ever saw, and yet he never won anything. Why? Because he lacked the heart to let his winnings stand."

Certainly, if the above exchange did take place, it seems to have proved prophetic for Company H, as the Confederates inflicted heavy losses on the Third Brigade during its first major battle on May 5, 1862. All told, five hundred of Hooker's men, including Woodbridge's own Lieutenant Berry, were wounded, killed or listed as missing at Williamsburg, Virginia, and as the battle raged amid a morass of rain and mud, perhaps the injured Berry was carried to a medical tent similar to the one then eighteen-year-old 5th New Jersey Volunteer infantryman Private Alfred Bellard describes in journal entries quoted by Meg Groeling in her *The Aftermath of Battle: The Burial of the Civil War Dead*: "The doctors were busy in probing for balls, binding up wounds, and cutting off arms and legs, a pile of which lay under the [amputation] table." The gruesome scene, later published in Bellard's book *Gone for a Soldier*, shows limbs scattered across the operating theater, filling shallow pits outside the tent and jostled in wheelbarrows used to cart them off. We might imagine the intense heartache and excruciating pain young Will Berry experienced, propped in some muddy corner of the tent, his ears ringing with the screams of strangers and, perhaps, screams from his own throat so loud he didn't recognize them as he said a final prayer for himself and the loving father he had left behind in Woodbridge.

When word reached Will's sisters, brothers and parents on the front steps of their pleasant home on the pleasant little street that now bears their name, the entire family must have broken down: we might imagine the heart-stricken wail from Margaret Inslee Berry (née Coddington) echoing down Rahway Avenue as Will's little brothers, Albion and Arthur, buried their

This circa 1893 Kurz & Allison print, *Battle of Williamsburg: Hancock's Charge*, depicts the hellish scene Lieutenant Berry confronted during Company H's first pitched battle. *Library of Congress.*

faces in their hands, and as his immediately younger brother, James, sobbing into his shirtsleeve, dashed down the tree-lined avenue to inform their sister Elizabeth and her husband, Lewis Browing. We can even imagine the old brick magnate himself, William H. Berry, whose long life had previously seen so much success—who, indeed, could have afforded Will a substitute dozens of times over—brushing away a tear and, feeling his heart about to explode, rushing into the house for a glass of water. Gone was the little boy he had once watched play outside the Strawberry Hill and Woodbridge Hall schoolhouses, the sixteen-year-old who had helped on the family farm and at the brick factory, and the promising young man who, just three years earlier, had won a citation from the New Jersey Agricultural Society for inventing a root cutter for chopping cattle feed.

In fact, as Troeger and McEwen describe it, when Will's body arrived home for burial, the entire town was in mourning. His funerary train car was adorned with black banners and crepe, and his coffin was escorted through town by his former compatriots in the Pike Guard, marching with their firearms held in reverse, to the Methodist church on Main Street. Then, the soldiers continued to stand vigil over his body on May 24, 1862, through his funeral at the First Presbyterian Church and his burial at the Methodist church, before finally wishing their fallen friend farewell as the first clod of white Woodbridge clay was shoveled onto the casket. No doubt, as they filed away from the ironically placid greenery of the Methodist cemetery, they realized neither their town nor the nation at large would ever be the same.

For their heroism at the Battle of Williamsburg, Company H sergeants Frederick Brill and John W. Flanigan, corporals Lewis F. Noe and John Sutton, and privates Dallas Noe, Patrick Kane and Charles C. and George W. Dally received military citations for bravery. Afterward, those still able to fight primarily skirmished with the rebels in various parts of Virginia until the Army of the Potomac made its equally ill-fated river crossing at Fredericksburg. According to most historians, the Union lost the element of surprise before the battle by awaiting the arrival of a pontoon bridge insisted upon by the army's commander, Major General Ambrose Burnside. As a result, by the time Hooker's men did cross the Rappahannock east of Fredericksburg, they came under nearly continuous fire from the already dug-in Confederates, then faced snipers from the town's windows, rooftops and alleyways. What's more, once they'd reached the other side of Fredericksburg, they were ordered to fix bayonets and charge through a furious barrage of bullets raining down from the heights opposite the river. Suffice it to say, Union casualties that day were staggering.

All told, Company H took part in twenty-eight battles, including nearly every major battle in the war's bloody Eastern Theater, from the Second Battle of Bull Run to Gettysburg to the Siege of Petersburg, while Company F, of Freehold's 28th New Jersey Volunteer Infantry, would see other parts of the same battlefields starting in 1862. What's more, twelve local men would join the U.S. navy, including Thomas McElroy, who was serving on the ironclad *Mound City* on Virginia's White River when he snatched Fort Charles's massive Confederate flag and sent it back home. According to Troeger and McEwen, one Woodbridge citizen then raised the captured "Stars and Bars" below the Stars and Stripes on the Pike House flagpole just before a Confederate attack on the *Mound City* killed every man aboard except McElroy and the ship's surgeon.

But, as the war raged on, the sheer numbers of combatants involved, their distance from the home front and the development of even deadlier, more impersonal means of killing would limit much of what we know anecdotally about Woodbridge's Civil War soldiers and sailors outside the greater national narrative. Indeed, many historians today claim the Union's siege of Petersburg, Virginia, under future president General Ulysses S. Grant, was the first instance of the brand of modern trench warfare that would become the norm half a century later during World War I. So, as casualty lists expanded late in the war, the carnage of these battles was so horrific that the personal experiences of individual soldiers frequently went unrecorded; after all, the traumatized survivors of these engagements may have sooner chosen to forget their hellish ordeals than relive them through storytelling. It's singularly indicative of the scars the Civil War left in the fabric of American culture that the greatest literary description of a Civil War battle, Stephen Crane's *The Red Badge of Courage*, was written not by a veteran but by a man who wasn't even born until seven years after the war ended.

BARONS AND BARRONS: INDUSTRIALIZATION, THE GILDED AGE, IMMIGRATION AND THE PROGRESSIVES

Even before the Civil War, Woodbridge had been building toward modern prosperity through mechanized production. Indeed, as early as the 1820s, residents like William Henry Berry, father of the much-grieved Lieutenant Berry, found the road to wealth wide open in the town. The key to such fortunes lay in the area's rich clay deposits found in the very same clay banks where, over a century later, fossilized dinosaur footprints would be found. Brought to the area in a series of alluvial deposits that shaped the region long enough ago for dinosaurs to leave a mark in it, according to an 1870 geological survey quoted by Troeger and McEwen, the clay seam originally stretched from Woodbridge to Perth Amboy.

When the town's first settlers arrived, then, they quickly discovered clay would be key to the town's success. In fact, the first indication of this came in 1670, just a year after the township's chartering, when Woodbridge's founders granted brick dealer John French fifteen acres and made him a

This 1871 painting by American folk artist James Bard depicts a typical domestic scene in late-1800s Woodbridge, with resident Charles Drake harnessing his horse, Jack. *Public domain.*

freeholder in exchange for his producing bricks and giving his neighbors first dibs on his wares over any outsider who might make a higher offer. Moreover, the town's colonial leaders also reserved several lots that would become clay banks for the "Molden Men," a term that, as Dally remarks, might well be a misspelling of "molding men," as in "those who mold bricks." Troeger and McEwen also report that Revolutionary War soldiers stationed in Perth Amboy used Woodbridge's unique white clay, which they called "fuller's earth," to dry-clean their breeches.

Thus, following the Revolutionary War, utilization of this major resource began in earnest when a local merchant shipped the first cargo of fire clay to Boston in 1816. Soon, as the advancements in eighteenth-century steam technology feeding Britain's Industrial Revolution spilled across the Atlantic, the old process of manually mining clay with pickaxes and shovels was replaced with early industrial-scale operations that used steam shovels to excavate gaping clay pits. The very first local company to do this was the Salamander Works, founded—as Troeger and McEwen speculate, by Gage Inslee and René Pardessus in 1825 where the Parker Press Park now

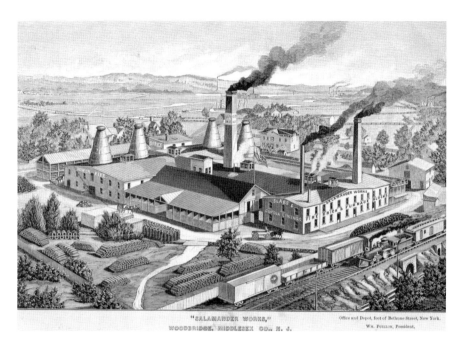

This postcard depicts the Woodbridge Salamander Works from an eastward rooftop vantage on Pearl Street—just as it looked around 1870 under William and Cornelius Poillon's ownership. *Public domain.*

sits—as a manufacturer of fireproof clay products such as bakers' ovens, slabs, furnace blocks and cupola linings. This was followed, in 1835, by the factory's expansion when clay dealer Peter Melick sold Pardessus twenty-three additional acres between Woodbridge and Metuchen. It wasn't long afterward that the Salamander Works began changing hands, first being sold to Frenchman Michel Lefoloun in 1837, then to Jules Decasse in 1842, then to Louis Decasse (likely Jules's son) in 1850 and, finally, to William Poillon and his son Cornelius in 1867. Eventually, in 1896, a fire destroyed the original Salamander Works, but Cornelius's wife, Clara Louise Poillon, and another relative, Mrs. Howard A. Pouillon, subsequently rebuilt, giving the facility a new kiln and moving their C.L. & H.A. Poillon Pottery Co. from Jersey City to Woodbridge, where it stood for several years before moving to Trenton.

The Salamander Works was especially renowned in the 1830s and 1840s for products that incorporated a "Rockingham glaze"—pioneered by the Rockingham Company of England, which specialized in colored pottery, especially red-brown wares. Among Salamander's most popular products

Founded in 1880, Carteret's Ichabod T. Williams & Sons Sawmill and Veneer Plant is evidence of how Woodbridge-area industrialization led to both boom and blight. *Library of Congress.*

in this vein were its unique dog-handled pitchers on which were depicted various designs, including a boar-hunting scene; a side-wheel steamer; and grapevines, fauns' heads, satyr masks and scrolls. Part mass-produced products, part art objects, these pieces became so popular that several still reside in the collections of the Smithsonian Institution, the New Jersey State Museum, the Henry Ford Museum and the Brooklyn Museum. But this is not the Salamander Works' only legacy. Other notable contributions to the art and science of pottery-making came from the Poillon family, especially the Poillon women, who were highly involved in the hand-decorated–china craze of the late nineteenth century. What's more, Clara herself developed gold and orange lusters and several matte and high-gloss glazes for use in her company's kitchenware and garden lines.

Due to these efforts, business boomed for the Salamander Works for the better part of a century, and it was soon joined by several other manufacturers of clay goods. Among these were Hampton Cutter & Sons, whose eponymous founder discovered several rare deposits of blue and white kaolin clays on his farm in 1845 and subsequently began shipping raw clay as far as New England, New York and Ohio with his sons Josiah C.

and William H. Cutter as well as with his son-in-law James Prall; William H. Berry & Co. firebrick factory, which is mentioned at greater length earlier in this chapter; Henry Mauer's Excelsior Fire-Brick & Clay Retort Works, which Mauer purchased in 1856 and which stood just over the Perth Amboy line in a seventy-five-acre section of the town now named for the German industrialist; the Dally Clay Pits, best known for owner Samuel Dally, who was highly regarded around town for his square dealing as well as for shuttering his business in 1864 to protest the large bonuses local U.S. army recruiters were offering his workers to enlist; C.W. Boynton & Co., which was founded in 1866 at the mouth of Woodbridge Creek in modern-day Sewaren by Maine native Cassimir Whitman Boynton; the M.D. Valentine & Bro. Brick Co., which was founded in 1866 by Mulford D. and James R. Valentine and which, after a fire gutted its original facility in 1956, would end up a division of the A.P. Green Fire Brick Co. of Mexico, Missouri, under whose aegis it would continue to operate until 1983; and, in brief, the Mutton Hollow Fire Brick Co.; the Raritan Hollow & Porous Brick Co.; the Ostrander Brick Works; G.G. Brinkman Co.; the Melick Bros. Clay Mining Co.; the Carteret Brick Works; the Florida Grove Co.; the Annes & Potter Fire Clay Co.; the Federal Terra Cotta Co.; the Atlantic Terra Cotta Co.; the National Fireproofing Co.; the McHose Clay Co.; J. Flood & Son; Ayres & Co.; and General Ceramics—as well as companies founded or cofounded by the Inslee, Crossman, Drummond, Almasi and Ryan families. Indeed, for a time between the Civil War and World War I, clay wasn't just a sector in Woodbridge's economy—it *was* the town's economy.

Further, the precipitous rise of manufacturing in Woodbridge was fed by the advent and rapid expansion of the nation's first superhighways—the railroads—in the mid-nineteenth century. Petitions to allow the railroads into the region were first sent to the New Jersey state legislature in 1827, and five years later, the New Jersey Rail Road & Transportation Co. (NJRR&T) built the first railroad into the greater Woodbridge area. Subsequently, in 1835, a stone bridge was built over the Rahway River to extend the line into Rahway, and a depot was built on Front Street in Rahway. Then, following two attempts to extend the railroad to Perth Amboy, a branch line into Woodbridge proper was constructed over nine years by the Perth Amboy & Woodbridge Railroad Co. after it made an initial public offering of twenty dollars per share in 1855 and found backers in Samuel Barron, James Valentine and Adam Lee, among others. From there, in 1869—the same year the Union Pacific and Central Pacific railroads met at Promontory Point to form the Transcontinental

Before Woodbridge's modern New Jersey Transit station was built on Pearl Street, residents rode the Perth Amboy & Woodbridge Railroad and Woodbridge Tramway lines—which were joined in 1869. *Michael Provance.*

Railroad—the Perth Amboy & Woodbridge Railroad line was joined to the Woodbridge Tramway Co.'s various trunk lines and expanded into outlying sections of Middlesex County. Finally, in 1873, a third local line was started by Central Railroad of New Jersey president John Taylor Johnston after he purchased the Perth Amboy & Elizabethport Railroad and constructed a Sewaren station on it, creating the line's first stop in Woodbridge after many years of merely passing through.

But, the problem was that all these rail companies initially saw each other as competitors. Thus, for instance, travelers headed from Jersey City toward Philadelphia, or vice versa, would have to get off at one terminal in New Brunswick and trek across town to the other. Such problems were rife in the early days of mass transit, as nearly every small town across the country invested in its own rail system, and competition between public and private companies frequently broke out into practical war, as it did between robber barons Cornelius Vanderbilt and Jay Gould during the "Erie War." Luckily, though, the public annoyance was sufficient in and of itself to join the NJRR&T Co.'s lines with those of the Camden & Amboy Railroad in

1867. Afterward, these lines were linked to the Delaware & Raritan Canal system as the United Canal & Rail Road Companies of New Jersey (or "Joint Companies"). They would continue operating under this umbrella until, confronted with precipitously declining freight rates, the company leased the entirety of its infrastructure to the Pennsylvania Rail Road (or "PRR"). Under PRR, then, the old Perth Amboy & Woodbridge Railroad Company became so popular that the company built a new, larger brick station in 1885 at Woodbridge's request.

Thus, as the introduction of the railroads roughly coincided with the boom in industrial manufacturing, quite a few Woodbridge residents amassed remarkable fortunes from shipping clay products throughout the country and the world. They used their newfound wealth to construct the many expansive Victorian structures that still catch the eye along Green Street and Amboy Avenue. For instance, with the fortune his clay pits generated, Hampton Cutter built the Cutter-Prall mansion in Amboy Avenue's Strawberry Hill section, while his son William and grandson Hampton II would each use their profits from the family business to build the two massive Victorian homes on the 100 block of Green Street. Meanwhile, in 1876, financier William E. Fink Jr. built the sprawling mansion at 44 Green Street that now serves as the Costello-Greiner Funeral Home. Between 1890 and 1900, New York customs broker William A.

Clay magnate William H. Cutter built the stunning Victorian at 123 Green Street in 1870; ironically, the 1880 census lists him as a "clay miner." *Historical Society of New Jersey.*

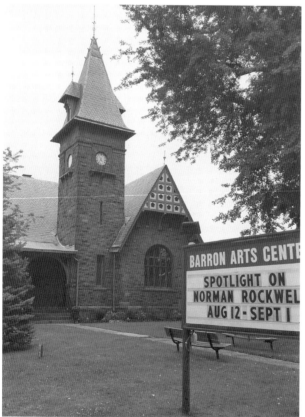

Above: In 1876, Woodbridge native William E. Fink Jr. built the Second Empire Victorian structure at 44 Green Street that now serves as the Costello-Greiner Funeral Home. *Michael Provance.*

Left: With a $50,000 bequest from his uncle Thomas, Dr. John Barron commissioned what is now the Barron Arts Center as Woodbridge's first library building. *Michael Provance.*

Osborn and M.D. Valentine & Bro. heir Howard Valentine built the historical homes that stand at 70 and 120 Green Street, respectively.

Moreover, the wealth amassed in Woodbridge during what American novelist Mark Twain dubbed the "Gilded Age" was also put to use in constructing various institutional and public buildings, such as Avenel's first PRR station, which once stood on the west side of the tracks; the First National Bank & Trust Building on Main Street, which was built in 1906 and long served as home to the city's chamber of commerce; and the gorgeous Barron Arts Center on Rahway Avenue, which originally housed the town's first free public library and which Civil War Union surgeon Dr. John C. Barron commissioned in 1875 on a parcel of land that was once part of the Barron homestead with $50,000 ($1.1 million in today's money) that his uncle, wealthy New York businessman and area philanthropist Thomas Barron, had bequeathed to the project in his will.

However, what Woodbridge's rich residents did when they weren't commissioning magnificent structures in town might be less appealing. According to the town's first historian, Joseph Dally, an "encrusted selfishness" had settled upon Woodbridge as it neared the nation's first centennial. This is evinced by the many fin-de-siècle pleasure palaces and

Constructed in 1906, the First National Bank and Trust building has served as headquarters for both the Middlesex Water Company and the Woodbridge Chamber of Commerce. *Woodbridge Township Historic Preservation Commission.*

retreats that area worthies constructed along the town's coastline, including the Sewaren House, constructed by Robert de Forest (railroad magnate John Taylor Johnston's son-in-law) in 1887, and the nearby Boynton Beach resort and Acker's Grove & Boat House, built around the same time by local porcelain manufacturer C.W. Boynton and canning-factory owner Henry Acker, respectively. Hence, while Woodbridge's leisure class made summer excursions back to Woodbridge from their homes in Manhattan, they were entirely cut off from the roiling mass of laborers whose work underpinned their fortunes. Indeed, many of the faceless, unsung men and women who dug up the clay and operated the kilns lived lives so unlike the charmed existences of Woodbridge's gentry that it's almost as if they lived in an altogether separate town.

As the Industrial Revolution took hold in Woodbridge, the town was flooded with the very same multitude of immigrants Emma Lazarus described in her 1883 poem "The New Colossus" as "huddled masses yearning to breathe free." Hailing predominantly from Ireland, Poland, Austria-Hungary and Italy, these new residents didn't speak the same tongue and, in most cases, didn't share the same religious views as those whose ancestors had arrived during the colonial period. Specifically, many of these newcomers were Catholic, and while there had been Catholics in Woodbridge as far back as the seventeenth century—when one Father Nicholas Gulick travelled to Woodbridge from Maryland to baptize resident Robert DuPoitiers and hold Mass at the home of first surveyor general Robert Vanquilion—there had also been a long, unofficial understanding among the town's "anti-Papist" majority that Woodbridge was a Protestant town. As a result, as Troeger and McEwen tell us, Catholics had to travel to Perth Amboy or Rahway to attend Mass, or find a priest who would hold services in their private homes, until 1865, when the first Catholic chapel, a wood-framed structure, was built on the south side of Main Street near Metuchen Avenue.

This chapel was succeeded in 1897 by the construction of the original St. James Church—precursor of today's modern St. James Church at the intersection of Main Street and Rahway Avenue—and would subsequently serve as the first site of the St. James School, run by the Sisters of Mercy.

Dedicated in 1968, today's St. James Roman Catholic Church replaced a Victorian precursor that long stood at the same location after the older building was moved there via tractor in 1924. *Michael Provance.*

After this, then, the proverbial dam seems to have broken, and many more immigrant and minority houses of worship appeared, including Woodbridge's Hungarian Reformed Church (built in 1904), the First Baptist Church (built in 1906), the Roman Catholic Church of Our Lady of Mount Carmel (built in 1920) and the Adath Israel Synagogue (built in 1948); Avenel's B'nai Jacob Synagogue (built in 1913) and St. Andrew's Roman Catholic Church (built in 1939); Fords's Slovak Presbyterian Church (built in 1926; now the Fords First Presbyterian Church) and St. Mary's Roman Catholic Church (built in 1929); Port Reading's St. Anthony of Padua Roman Catholic Church (built in 1914); and Colonia's St. John Vianney Roman Catholic Church (completed in 1968).

Of course, the hurtful truth is that speaking, looking and worshipping differently didn't help the immigrant community—or, for that matter, the African American community—gain respect and equal treatment from the affluent, lily-white owners of the factories where they worked. Indeed, for all of the nineteenth century and most of the early twentieth century, even wealthy Catholics were tacitly snubbed by their Protestant neighbors; anti-Catholic attitudes would not change until the middle of the twentieth century, when Catholic celebrities like Frank Sinatra and President John F.

Kennedy made Catholicism more widely accepted. And how much worse for those of faiths or denominations, appearances and languages that set them even further outside the accepted norm!

The end result of all this bigotry was that those whom Woodbridge's WASPs perceived as "subhuman" (to use a hateful term of that period) were segregated into outlying communities closer to the ash-covered, smog-enshrouded factories and ever-widening maws of the clay pits, where some worked for up to sixteen hours per day for nearly nothing. The mood of these poor souls, then, was understandably despairing, as evinced by a song, "The Dreary Sand Hills," which was popular among Irish immigrants and was recalled in 1931 by resident Ruth Wolk, who had once heard police chief Patrick W. Murphy sing it. The lyrics, referring to Fords—which was then called "the Sand Hills" for its clay and sand pits—is worth replicating here, from Troeger and McEwen, for a sense of the period:

> *I came to the Sand Hills to get me a job;*
> *I met Billy Barr, and he sent me to Bob,*
> *Said, "If he won't take you, I'm sure that Howe will*
> *Let you dig clay on the dreary Sand Hills.*
>
> *"There's Francis Ostrander, who owns a clay mine,*
> *Pfeiffer and Edgar and Bob Valentine.*
> *But, if they don't offer, go down to Crow Mills,*
> *Cause clay's all the same on the dreary Sand Hills.*
>
> *"And then there's Tom Egan, who keeps a Bee Hive.*
> *He says, 'You'll need whiskey to keep you alive.'*
> *I got it this morning; it's fresh from the still.*
> *It's the best thing we've got on the dreary Sand Hills."**

As this song shows, life was mean for Woodbridge's working class, and it remained so well into the twentieth century, as did attitudes toward immigrants. In fact, as Bond relates, evidence of such prejudices arises well

---

*The One and Only Footnote: As presented by Troeger and McEwen, these lyrics were fraught with metrical inconsistencies, which likely resulted from some oral historian's misremembering them. Thus, to approximate something closer to the original that was likely sung in Woodbridge's nineteenth-century clay pits, my version is slightly modified to retain a strict ballad meter; interested readers may refer to Troeger and McEwen's *Woodbridge: New Jersey's Oldest Township* for what I consider the less-likely version recorded in the town's annals.

Though Carteret is now an independent town, its 109-year-old Ukrainian Orthodox congregation and St. Demetrius Cathedral stand as a testament to Woodbridge's nineteenth-century diversity. *Farragutful.*

into the twentieth century with, for instance, both local and national papers publishing scathingly patronizing coverage of Woodbridge Hungarian immigrant Theresa Czinkota's trial for witchcraft in the 1930s. At that time, no less than *Time* magazine mocked Czinkota and her neighbors, and the local *Leader Journal*'s verbose headline was no less sardonic: "Scene of 'Old Salem' Re-Enacted in Local Police Court Yesterday with Preposterous 'Witch' Tale." As for the story itself, apparently Czinkota's cousin and next-door neighbor Mary Rottenhofer, along with fellow immigrants Theresa Kayla, Gertrude Mutter and Rose Cseptser, accused Czinkota of witchcraft, perhaps hoping the police court that heard the case would enforce a state law, first passed in 1668, that made witchcraft a capital offense.

According to Bond's summary, Mutter alleged that, from the vantage of one of Rottenhofer's windows, she saw "Mrs. Czinkota [bend] down, her head changed into a dog's" and that she witnessed Czinkota grow "big bumps on her back." The dialogue Bond records from period papers between presiding Judge Arthur Brown and Czinkota's accusers is a telling indication of attitudes even as late as 1936:

> *Brown: Are you a Catholic, Mrs. Mutter?*
> *Mutter: I am a good Catholic.*
> *B: Do you actually believe that there is such a thing as a witch?*
> *M: Seeing is believing.*
> *B: Don't you know that the Catholic Church does not recognize witchcraft and that a good Catholic, therefore, does not believe in witchcraft?*
> *M: Yes—But I saw it with my own eyes.*
> *B: Did you ever see any pictures about witchcraft?*
> *M: I only go when Shirley Temple plays.*

In delivering his decision, Judge Brown was quoted as saying (again, as per Bond), "In the case of Mrs. Rottenhofer, it is my opinion that she should have a mental examination by a psychiatrist." We must remember, too, that newspapers and magazines in Woodbridge and across the United States, at the time, were reporting all this presumably as comic relief for predominantly WASP audiences. Of course, today, from a much more enlightened vantage, it's obvious that the women's accusation against Czinkota can't bear

Right and opposite: Edison's current Our Lady of Peace Roman Catholic church and school were completed in 1955, but many Fords Catholics have belonged to its congregation since 1919. *Brewbooks.*

weight in light of logical thinking and that, as Bond notes, some falling out between Czinkota and Rottenhofer was probably at the heart of the matter. Clearly, though, Czinkota's accusers truly believed she was a witch, and this was given no credence; rather, the courts and media of the period took the opportunity presented by these accusations to lampoon the women and the wider immigrant community both in Woodbridge and across the nation. Never mind that distant relatives of those laughing in 1936 had gone so far as to hang their neighbors on charges of witchcraft less than three hundred years earlier.

As per Troeger and McEwen, Woodbridge's workers did try to combat their ill treatment. The first labor strike began on June 19, 1866, and involved organized bands of workers marching from clay pit to clay pit enlisting sympathetic workers and intimidating scabs (i.e., those willing to work during a strike). Leon McElroy (via Troeger and McEwen) claims the peaceful protest devolved into mob violence when marchers wielding clubs and guns ran amok in the township's streets. However, we might take this particular report of rioting with a grain of salt, as companies often hired agents provocateurs to infiltrate labor groups and orchestrate riots—thereby setting local townspeople and state and local law enforcement against nonviolent demonstrations. McElroy's more reliable statements on the strike, in contrast, claim that labor leaders met on June 25, 1866, to discuss pooling their resources if the strike was forced to continue into the next three months and that the meeting was broken up by the Middlesex County sheriff and his constables and deputies. Driven into the woods, then, many strikers found themselves arrested and held at Samuel Dally's house until mid-August 1866, when they were forced to return to work for their old wages.

Afterward, as McElroy relates, the town's clay magnates voluntarily gave workers a raise—from $1.50 to $1.75 per day. To put this in perspective, even with this raise, the workers were still making a meager $29.75 per day in today's money—the equivalent of only $10,858.75 a year—if a worker worked all 365 days. Worse, when workers again insisted on better pay during an 1873 strike, their protest was quickly squelched by the Woodbridge Clay Miners' Association, a group of local clay-pit and factory owners formed in 1866 during a meeting at the Pike House between Charles M. Dally, Isaac Inslee, J. Mattison Melick, Jacob R. Crossman and others. Considering when it was founded, it is not unlikely that this association was formed in response to the 1866 strike and that it might have very well served as a wage- and rate-setting cabal, as well.

Thus, to combat the depredations of industrialization in the late nineteenth century, the Progressive Party in Woodbridge, spearheaded by Colonia resident Mary Hart Pattison, began taking political action. Among the Progressives' many "radical" demands were the eight-hour workday and the minimum wage, woman suffrage, free public schools, public police and fire departments, laws banning child labor, safe housing and working conditions, food-safety and -quality requirements, a breakup of the trusts and monopolies that fixed prices and manipulated markets, and a ban on alcohol (predominantly viewed as an immigrant vice). As a testament to the movement's success, only one of these points—the ban on alcohol—would seem radical today (because of Prohibition's failure in the 1920s). Believe it or not, unlike many other communities at the end of the nineteenth century, Woodbridge was actually well ahead of the proverbial curve in several of the above-listed areas long before the 1890s.

Say what we might about the often inhumane treatment of minorities and the poor by members of Woodbridge's WASP elite, their ancestors did provide for public schooling at the town's inception, securing one hundred acres of untaxed public land for "the maintenance of a free school" in the township's 1669 charter and hiring the town's first schoolteacher, James

While their workers were predominantly Catholic, many of Woodbridge's elite, including the Boyntons, Coddingtons, Harneds and Inslees, attended the First Congregational Church, which was built in 1876. *Michael Provance.*

Built in 1910, the J.J. Bitting Brewing Company started as a Progressive Era coal and feed depot; Woodbridge's government distributed necessities from the company's back lot. *Michael Provance.*

Fullerton, on March 3, 1689. And, while it is true that later freeholders would raid the school's coffers to purchase war bonds during the Revolution, they would eventually restore the money and even add to the school's funding with a dog tax in 1789, by which time this endowment for "schooling poor peoples' children" had already provided the town with its first schoolhouse on Strawberry Hill, as well as a schoolhouse in Rahway.

Moreover, the town's early residents also provided for a safety net for the poor, assessing the first poor tax in 1709, out of which "keepers of the poor" were reimbursed their expenses for housing and feeding the town's indigent. Plus, during the colonial period, the town provided public funding for a pound (in 1674), a jail (in 1675), a constable and even a dogcatcher. For these innovations, Woodbridge residents can feel a great deal of pride. After all, it wasn't until 1918 that every other community across the country had compulsory school-attendance laws.

In the wake of the Industrial Age's worst depredations and the Gilded Age's worst excesses, then, several prominent Woodbridge-area residents worked to build on these early milestones. For instance, as far back as 1817, Middlesex County assemblyman James Parker, a relative of the Woodbridge printer, introduced the first legislation to provide state funding for education. In 1871, to combat the problem of some neighborhoods having less school funding, Woodbridge's various neighborhood school districts were consolidated into the Woodbridge Area School District, whose board was led by local clay millionaire William H. Berry. Subsequently, the first of the new district's school buildings, School One, was completed in 1877 on land purchased from James Valentine just a year earlier. This was followed by the construction of over two dozen other school buildings throughout the township, including Ross Street's historic School Eleven, which opened as Woodbridge High School in 1911 and has served the community as a middle school since 1956.

Meanwhile, Woodbridge began providing greater protection for public safety by naming Patrick "Big Paddy" Cullinane its first policeman in 1896, a year after appointing him constable, and by purchasing the first horse-drawn fire company wagon sometime around 1915. Troeger and McEwen are especially detailed in their description of how the first police

Opened on Barron Avenue in 1911, Woodbridge High School is just one of over two dozen public-school buildings constructed in Woodbridge during the Progressive Era. *Michael Provance.*

Above: First organized in 1897, Woodbridge's fire department dedicated its first School Street firehouse in 1901; today's firehouse, built in 1969, sits on the same site. *Michael Provance.*

Left: This memorial to Woodbridge's firefighters commemorates their 122 years of service to the town; indeed, from 1897 to 1937, the force consisted entirely of volunteers. *Michael Provance.*

officer kept the town safe, saying, "[Cullinane] could lift a suspect by the collar and transport him single-handedly to the lockup." They also note, however, that most of Cullinane's duties entailed keeping vagrants out of town, preventing loitering and catching unlicensed dogs; it was only after the state allocated police funding in 1911 that Woodbridge's police received pay raises and uniforms and their promotions and salaries were based on a merit system.

Moreover, under Pattison's guidance as both a committee member of the state Progressive Party and president of the New Jersey Federation of Women's Clubs, local reformers opened the State Housekeeping Experiment Station next door to Pattison's home with the goal of lowering the cost of living, alleviating the shortage of domestic workers and removing the endless toil of housework. While this project might seem almost humorously small-potatoes today, at the station's opening in 1910, it was quite radical in aiming to give women more free time, thereby allowing them to take on greater roles in public life. Thus, in conducting time-motion studies for household tasks and testing various sources of energy and appliances—all of which Pattison describes in her 1914 book *The Principles of Domestic Engineering*—the station's staff were taking the first steps toward greater gender equality.

As for the other reforms demanded by Progressives, many of them would have to be addressed on the state and federal levels. There were, after all, just too many societal ills for local reformers to address them all. But just imagine life in Woodbridge if you had to send your children to a one-room schoolhouse reliant on your neighborhood's taxes alone, or if there were neither police nor firefighters to protect your home, and it's easy to see how great an impact the town's Progressives continue to have on our lives today.

CHAPTER V

MODERN LIVING

Woodbridge from the Great War to Today

"On or about December 1910," British essayist and novelist Virginia Woolf famously wrote, "human character changed." And, to some extent, despite Woolf's admittedly arbitrary date, this is true. For, in the period between 1910 and 1950, the scale of human life changed: wars were fought with weapons that would have made the demons in Dante Alighieri's *Inferno* drool, economic collapses became so immense that they created worldwide mass starvation and homelessness and technological advances that would have seemed like witchcraft in 1669 entered every American household. As a result, for those who had spent their childhoods amid the relative idyll of nineteenth-century Woodbridge, the uncharted territory of the twentieth century marked a sea change: the foes were no longer necessarily your neighbors; they just as likely lived thousands of miles away.

Yet, as many contemporary historians have remarked, the shift Woolf observed was especially jarring for Americans. For, after the second decade of the twentieth century, the piecemeal, as-needed U.S. foreign policies of yesteryear became stances toward ongoing international struggles, even as regional differences between Americans became increasingly less pronounced due to advances in mass communications and retail marketing. Unlike its first two and a half centuries, then, Woodbridge's twentieth and twenty-first centuries would see it become less of an isolated community and more the suburb of New York City we know today, as the big issues of the next one hundred years played out in Washington and elsewhere.

This page: These two photos of Main Street—taken at opposite ends of the twentieth century—show just how much Woodbridge has changed in only one hundred years. *Top, Woodbridge Township Historic Preservation Society; bottom, Michael Provance.*

The Enemy Beyond:
The World Wars, the Roaring '20s
and the Great Depression

As most historians have noted, World Wars I and II were arguably the same hellish conflict separated by twenty years of boom and bust. What's more, because they occurred in theaters well beyond Woodbridge's boundaries, their history is such a matter of national and global record that there is little left for a local history to treat. That said, it's still reasonable to discuss those Woodbridge residents who fought in these conflicts—insomuch as records are available—and the many efforts folks on the home front made to help their brothers, sons, fathers and husbands safely return. But, the main problem with giving an accurate account of Woodbridge history during World War I, specifically, is that so little local history comes down to us. Starting a local newspaper is always a gamble, and during the brief but crucial period of America's involvement in the war (1817–18), no local papers existed. The *Independent Hour, Weekly Register* and *Woodbridge News*, which had served the town and its neighborhoods in the 1870s and 1890s, were already shuttered, and it was not until after the war, in 1919, that the *Woodbridge Independent* started its twenty-year run.

What little comes down to us, then, is mostly information compiled by Troeger and McEwen in the 1990s. For example, they note that the first act of Woodbridge's local authorities when the United States declared war was to form the Home Defense League (HDL). This group, organized by Colby Dill, E.H. Boynton and Andrew Keyes, was to act as a local militia to defend the town against invasion. Naturally, the idea of an invasion of Woodbridge might sound strange today. But we have to remember that, in World War I, Germany *did* boast a powerful navy with plenty of dreaded U-boats regularly slipping in and out of Britain's blockade of the North Sea. We also have to remember that Woodbridge was still a major manufacturing center at the time and that Sewaren sits on the Arthur Kill, which feeds directly into the Atlantic. Consequently, the HDL was something of a full-fledged military unit of middle-aged men who wore uniforms, carried firearms and drilled in case the Central Powers made a run at their clay.

As for what the Germans might have targeted, in its drive to arm General John J. Pershing's expeditionary force in France, the federal government had contracted the Federal Terra Cotta Company, located on Cutters Dock Road, to supply the army with terra cotta dummy bombs. As Troeger and McEwen record, in 2001, the Historical Association of Woodbridge and the Cornelius Low House/Middlesex County Museum in Piscataway discovered 150 terra cotta dummy bombs manufactured during the period and buried where the factory once stood. Discarded as "wasters" because they had cracked during the firing process, each recovered bomb weighs eighteen and a half pounds (sans fins, nose and tail plug), is open at both ends and is shaped (per Elias Holzman, via Troeger and McEwen) "like a slim football, almost two-feet long with a maximum diameter of almost six inches." Uncracked dummies, created by Federal Terra Cotta Company workers like Woodbridge resident Severino Fiorentini, primarily figured into training runs for the army's fledgling air force: a crew would drop a dummy filled with flour or powdered plaster onto a target while in flight, then instructors would gauge the crew's accuracy based on the white spot the dummy left when it exploded.

However, the greatest impact those at home had during World War I took the form of the many charities and public-aid organizations they created to help the war's veterans. For instance, in Colonia, several local women had organized the Mercy Committee earlier in the war to send relief to war-ravaged Europe; thus, once the American army returned from France, the committee was able to easily shift its focus to aiding and rehabilitating Woodbridge's veterans. Meanwhile, in the same neighborhood, U.S. General Army Hospital No. 3 stood on two hundred acres leased from resident Charles D. Freeman when he and its future director, fellow Colonia resident Dr. Edward Houdlett Albee, met on a train to New York. The hospital, opened in 1918, boasted 110 barracks-like buildings, each with 18 single-story wards, a telephone exchange, a central heating plant, five mess halls and kitchens, a swimming pool, libraries and even its own newspaper, *Over Here*. The hospital's core mission was to treat returning soldiers for orthopedic injuries under the direction of Dr. Albee, an orthopedic specialist, and of the six thousand soldiers treated at the facility, only seventeen died; in fact, before it closed in October 1919, the vast majority of the hospital's patients would make a full recovery after undergoing cutting-edge bone-graft treatments developed by Dr. Albee.

Moreover, when local servicemen returned to Woodbridge, city hall voted to approve funds for a town-wide celebration held on November 12, 1918. In the proceeding weeks, the town also sent resolutions to families of the fallen (including Antonio Coppola, Lawrence Ballard, Stanley Carlson, Ira C. Dunn, Charles S. Farrell Jr., Edward M. Kelly, Charles Marty, Joseph Resch, Stephen Rocsi, William J. Senson and Thomas Terp), presented scrolls to all returning soldiers and sailors and began planning a memorial.

This early-1900s view of Main Street shows Woodbridge's Methodist church building—originally erected with a spire in 1870—before a massive fire gutted it in 1954. *Woodbridge Township Historic Preservation Society.*

What the town didn't suspect, in the war's aftermath, was how many of those returning would soon find themselves under attack from a far more lethal enemy: Spanish flu. A particularly virulent strain of the common flu, the virus hit hardest among people between the ages of eighteen and forty. The first mention in local record of the flu appeared in the March 21 issue of the *Woodbridge Independent*, which began publishing the same year, during the spring after Woodbridge's World War I veterans returned home. By then, the illness had mostly run its course, but in the two articles published in the *Independent*, we find mention of how the flu's effects were exacerbated by a shortage of doctors due to the war effort and that retail druggists in Woodbridge remained open at night during the epidemic (unheard of before the advent of Walgreens and CVS); what's more, in reporting on a nurse hired by the town's board of health, an open letter by health inspector L.E. Potter reveals that many local families suffered the loss of their breadwinners, and a March 28, 1919, issue shows a photograph of the graves of one hundred servicemen who died from the Spanish flu while convalescing in Devonshire, England.

Though Woodbridge demolished the Memorial Municipal Building erected in 1924 to honor its World War I vets, the new municipal building is still "Dedicated to Veterans." *Michael Provance.*

These brief accounts hardly do justice to the scope of an epidemic that, according to Richard V.N. Ginn's *The History of the U.S. Army Medical Service Corps*, killed 30 million people worldwide. Indeed, in an interview that town historian Brenda Velasco conducted in 2010 with Julie Ficso Rosmos and Barbara Rosmos Estok, survivor Julie Rosmos recalled that "so many people died off like flies" in Keasbey during the pandemic that her family walked all the way to Elizabeth to escape the disease. Worse, in the same interview, Velasco observes that many of the Spanish flu's victims died within three days of showing symptoms. No doubt, the precipitous spread of the disease in Woodbridge and elsewhere was due, in no small part, to the fact that millions of soldiers were returning home just as it hit. That said, it is an irony of history that (according to a 1919 surgeon general's report titled *Excerpts on the Influenza and Pneumonia Pandemic of 1918*) "the influenza epidemic was very mild [at Colonia's General Hospital No. 3] and there were less than 100 cases, very few being serious. Of interest from an epidemiological standpoint was the unusually small number of cases of influenza, this no doubt being due to the strict quarantine maintained from the beginning and enforced after the State quarantine was lifted." Apparently, with Dr. Albee in charge, the safest place in Woodbridge during the pandemic was the very same hospital hosting the town's largest population of returning servicemen.

✷⟫⟫✕⟪⟪

IN THE TWENTY YEARS between World Wars I and II, Americans became both shockingly rich and miserably poor. In 1924, Woodbridge residents ushered in the boom by building a new Memorial Municipal Building to replace their old town hall, and in 1926, they opened the Woodbridge Speedway on the site where Woodbridge's modern high school stands today. Apparently, many members of the town's growing middle class had the free time to watch cars—like the Miller Majestic Special and the Fronty Special—tear around the "World's Fastest Half-Mile Race Track," their muffler-less engines growling so loudly that residents often reported hearing them as far away as Main Street.

However, as Bond has observed, after Congress passed the Eighteenth Amendment on January 16, 1919, crime also rose in Prohibition-era Woodbridge, as what American author and Princeton graduate F. Scott Fitzgerald called the "Jazz Age" raged. For instance, at one speakeasy owned by Louis Majaveta in the predominantly Hungarian section of Fulton Street, a May 1922 raid headed by New Jersey chief Prohibition agent Samuel H. Cone saw Mrs. Majaveta claw and bite one agent and tear the clothes off another; meanwhile, just down the street, agents netted Steve Kristoff and his illicit whiskey still, seizing thirteen quarts of moonshine, two gallons of mash and a barrel of "poor quality" wine. Yet these busts were chump change compared with another incident involving Woodbridge resident Julius Magyar: along with two other men, Magyar attempted to smuggle seventy cases of liquor into Woodbridge in June 1924 using a motorboat. When U.S. Revenue agents gave chase in their own boat, according to the *Trenton Evening Times* (via Bond), the G-men fired as many as fifty shots at Magyar's craft, setting its engine ablaze.

What's more, in inadvertently acting as a boon to organized crime, Prohibition also increased the prevalence of other social ills after the U.S. stock market suddenly crashed on October 29, 1929. For, despite the repeal of the Eighteenth Amendment via the Twenty-First Amendment on December 5, 1933, the doomed experiment of Prohibition had given Depression-era criminals the impetus to organize. Their infrastructure, created from rum-running, was already in place to facilitate prostitution and gambling operations throughout Woodbridge. Thus, in a decade that saw as

Formally opened in 1927, the fabled Woodbridge Speedway began in 1926 as a dirt track; it was subsequently replaced with wooden and, finally, oiled-dirt tracks. *Woodbridge Township Historic Preservation Society.*

many as half of working-age adults unemployed, many area residents who would never have done so otherwise became desperate enough to go rogue. For example, Richard Cavalarro and several others were arrested during a 1934 raid on Cavalarro's home, where the Fords resident was operating a gambling establishment, and Hopelawn resident Mary Martha Nyers was arrested for prostitution in February 1938.

As Bond also notes, town authorities attempted to directly attack these ills, as when Woodbridge chief of police Patrick Murphy focused his force of forty-one officers and their modern fingerprinting and photography departments on shuttering even the smallest mom-and-pop gambling establishment, telling the *Woodbridge Independent* on August 28, 1931, "The gambling den, the disorderly house and the slot machine are the most common forms of lawlessness attempted…[and] the commercialized gambling racket is smashed wherever it appears." At the same time, more enlightened residents, like then-Mayor William A. Ryan, took aim at the root of the problem—poverty—of which such crimes were merely

Today, the numerous circuses and carnivals held in the mid-1930s as fundraisers for a town stadium are little-remembered features of Depression-era life in Woodbridge. *Public domain.*

symptoms; as Troeger and McEwen explain, Ryan addressed Depression-era poverty early, appointing a committee in 1930 to investigate the downturn's effects on the town. The committee found that those hit hardest were people associated with the town's clay industry, which had been on the brink since 1920, when clay was discovered in Tennessee, Kentucky, Pennsylvania and Ohio—all states whose railroad freight rates were much lower than New Jersey's. Based on these findings, the township created the Citizens' Committee for the Relief of the Unemployed and Needy, headed by John E. Breckenridge.

Of course, compounding the town's woes, the crash of '29 had sparked a run in March 1930 on First National Bank & Trust that drained it of over $1 million. Though the bank's board of directors subsequently put up $75,000 to keep the bank open, it was forced to close on November 30, 1931, after federal bank examiners found it didn't have the funds to operate. As the *Woodbridge Independent* reported on December 18, 1931, the bank had almost remained open, as it had secured promises on Sunday, November 29, 1931, from the Middlesex Bankers Association to cover the differences in its balance sheets. However, this plan came to naught the following morning, when it was discovered that one liability had not been reported to the association in time for the organization to provide the additional capital needed to cover the debt. As a result, First National Bank & Trust had to shut its doors at 8:00 a.m. to prevent a criminal liability that would have ensued had it begun accepting deposits.

In the end, though, First National Bank & Trust wasn't alone. Of all the banks that existed in Woodbridge before the crash, only Fords National

Bank survived. This created an issue for the town's businesses, which were already suffering from slackening sales because they had fewer opportunities to secure loans to expand or continue operations. The domino effect then hit the township itself, as fewer workers and businesses meant a shrinking tax base, which in turn meant layoffs among the city's municipal employees. To stem this vicious cycle, Mayor Ryan implored private citizens and local businesses to buy small-denomination municipal bonds, or "Baby Bonds," while the Woodbridge Township Taxpayers Association proposed a series of cost-cutting measures starting in 1932. But the simple fact was that, without jobs, there weren't enough consumers to support the town's businesses, and without businesses, there wasn't enough tax money to keep the government running.

To combat this issue in towns across the country, President Franklin Delano Roosevelt's administration created the Civilian Conservation Corps, which came to Woodbridge in 1932 and quickly began hiring the town's young men to maintain its parks. Meanwhile, on the local level, resident John H. Love organized the three-day Woodbridge Township National Recovery Exposition, at which local businesses could show off their wares in the hopes of bolstering sales. Other local groups that assisted in the town's recovery included Colonia Citizens Inc., which first met in 1932 and worked to assist Colonia residents by marketing their homemade goods while also publishing Colonia's first newspaper, the *Colonia Sun*. Yet, the township still confronted shortages into 1934, as Mayor August F. Greiner took office, prompting Greiner to make taxpayers a deal: if they paid their 1933 taxes in cash by January 31, the township would waive all outstanding interest owed. What's more, Greiner refinanced Woodbridge's defaulted municipal bonds and insisted that businesses with government contracts hire unemployed locals rather than importing cheap labor from out of state.

As a result, the town avoided bankruptcy, and by the fall of 1935, local construction was on the mend. To be sure, this didn't end the Depression in Woodbridge—as shown by the closing of the Speedway in 1938—but the number of residents listed as Works Progress Administration employees did steadily decline, and in 1935, the Reo Diner on Main Street—which had opened a year before the crash, in 1928, and would later become famous for WOR radio personality Bob Grant's catchphrase, "Meet me at the Reo"—changed its name from "The Hy-Way Diner" to "The Reo" to install a new neon sign (without breaking the bank with too many letters) and also became the first diner in New Jersey to stay open twenty-four

Technically, Woodbridge's WPAers beautified Edison's Roosevelt Park. But who needs the creepiness of *Light Dispelling Darkness* with Pablo's Grill's 2009 donation of this piece to Heards Brook Park? *Michael Provance.*

This page: An institution in Woodbridge, Amboy Avenue's Reo Diner is also a New Jersey landmark as the first all-night diner in a state known for its all-night diners. *Public domain.*

hours a day. Moreover, in 1937, the Woodbridge National Bank opened its doors, signaling that the worst was over. New projects, like the all-volunteer Woodbridge Emergency Squad and the Woodbridge Alumni Golden Bears, a semi-professional football team, formed in 1937 and 1940, respectively, showing that more and more residents were again enjoying free time and the financial security necessary to take on projects that didn't bring home the proverbial bacon.

As World War II swept across Europe and Asia, Woodbridge was again on the upswing. Its attention was also beginning to turn toward conflicts across the globe, as Austria, Czechoslovakia, Poland and France fell to Nazi Germany in quick succession. Despite the antiwar fervor then in many parts of the country, the people of Woodbridge knew and accepted the inevitability of America's involvement, with 3,780 area men between twenty-one and thirty-five years of age signing up for the selective service in October 1940, more than a full year before Pearl Harbor and the United States' entry into the war. Further, in August 1940 and February 1941, the township authorized the Home Defense Fund and Woodbridge Defense Council, respectively, following Governor A. Harry Moore's directive that all New Jersey towns do so.

Perhaps the reason for this fervor was that Woodbridge was already contending with the idea of foreign threats. After all, not long after the town's massive enlistment, on November 12, 1940, residents were roused from bed in the wee hours by an explosion at Port Reading's United Railway Signal Company. The blast shook downtown Woodbridge to its foundations, not only wiping the United Railway Signal Company from the map but also taking the Middlesex Water Company and several nearby homes with it, while among the dead were Middlesex Water Company foreman Dominick LaPenta and eight signal workers. Moreover, despite the fact that the United Railway Signal Company held no government contracts at the time, this level of devastation prompted several national and local newspapers to attribute the explosion to foreign saboteurs. Whatever the reason (which was never determined) for the United Railway Signal Company explosion, when President Roosevelt addressed a joint session of Congress with his "day that will live in infamy" speech on December 7, 1941, Woodridge was already preparing for war.

Following Congress's formal declaration of war, local authorities quickly divided the town into sixteen air-defense zones—basing them on existing fire districts—and installed air-raid sirens. Meanwhile, the Defense Council, in coordination with New Jersey's State Defense Council, organized squads of local air-raid wardens, auxiliary firemen, couriers, drivers and messengers, while other council subcommittees and area organizations started blood drives, first-aid and emergency road-repair services, rationing committees, surgical supply collections, salvage drives, public-information outlets and a whole host of other wartime ventures. Moreover, the town also began blackout drills in April 1942, and the following May, its traditional Memorial Day radio broadcast was transmitted nationwide, highlighting the town as a "Typical American Community." As part of the program, Mayor Greiner spoke at the First Presbyterian Church cemetery, saying "We are ready to join our sister communities whenever called."

Soon, however, the Defense Council was forced to relinquish some local oversight over the war effort when the list of rationed items grew so long that it required a full-fledged rationing board to oversee its implementation. Such an organization was therefore created under the direction of Charles E. Gregory, managing editor of Woodbridge's *Independent-Leader*, and as part of the board's responsibilities, it was tasked with equitable distribution of rationed items not only in Woodbridge and its neighborhoods but also in Carteret and Metuchen. Included on the ration list were sugar, butter, meat, canned goods, tires, fuel oil, gasoline and rubber footwear, and the system devised for rationing entailed purchasing such items using stamps from a federal ration booklet; shoppers were required, whenever making purchases, to present their stamps, which the ration board meted out. Booklets included as few stamps for each class of item as possible based on the rationing board's calculation of how many items could be sold without creating shortages. Local businesses would then turn their collected stamps over to the board so it could guard against counterfeiting and keep track of what supplies had been allocated.

And yet, Woodbridge's greatest contribution to the war effort was, of course, the many young men who joined up and sacrificed themselves in Europe and the Pacific. Hundreds of letters passed between these men and their families, and in many cases, this was the last communication their parents, wives and children would ever receive from them. Moreover, these letters offer some of the best glimpses we have of what Woodbridge's sailors, soldiers and airmen faced in their fights against global totalitarianism, as evinced by the following excerpt from an August 5, 1943, letter sent by

Bombardier Albert "Albee" Leffler to his friend Art Spoon in Sewaren. In it, Albee describes army life in North Africa just days before he was reported missing in action; the *Fords Beacon* published the letter on November 19, 1943, roughly a month after its receipt:

> *Well, to begin with, I have been over here for seven months, could be longer. I'm here in North Africa, and all I can say is that it is too long. I'm over here as a combat crew member and have been in action for about six months. I'm a Bombardier, and so far, I'm still kicking and biting the old dirt. Dear old North Africa—we fought like hell for it—but now we have it, and I don't know yet what they want it for. I wouldn't trade Sewaren for all of Africa.... The weather was hot and dusty for a long time, and we didn't see rain for about six months—we have rain now and it's about time. Our food consists of "C" rations which [are] very good, but we're still trying to find out for whom.*

The following month, the *Independent-Leader* published an update on Albee in the form of a letter Staff Sargent Nate Bernstein wrote to Albee's mother on November 21, 1943:

> *I received word from my sister that you have received word from the War Department regarding Albee and that he in missing. I was not able to write you before about it. Otherwise I would have done so. However, I have a bit of encouraging news: although one can never be too sure about these things, after the crew [of Albee's flight] went down in enemy waters, several planes saw all of the men in a raft, and it is altogether possible that he is now in the hands of the enemy as a prisoner of war.*

Later, hope for Albee's survival was further encouraged when his parents received the following letter (reprinted in the May 12, 1944, issue of the *Independent-Leader*) from another son, Walter "Bud" Leffler, who was then stationed in Texas:

> *I started my classes yesterday and [there're] about 30 of us officers in it and two enlisted men from overseas. It sure is funny. One of the enlisted men is a staff sergeant, and when he heard my name called in rollcall this morning he came over to talk to me after class. Come to find out he's from Al's squadron overseas and had just come back as he'd finished his 40 missions. He knew Al real well and used to pitch on Al's softball team over*

there. His name is Sgt. Quine, and he's from Denver, Colorado. He said that he remembered when Al's ship was shot down and that all the crew were in the lifeboat, They'd sent out some Navy planes the next day, but they were gone and they figured that they had been picked up by the enemy. He figured that it was about Al's 24th mission.... Later on, while this Quine was still in Africa, one of their officers who had been taken prisoner, escaped from a German prison camp and returned to the squadron. He claimed that he had seen Al and the rest of the crew in the same prison camp. So, you see: Al was taken prisoner, and I sure hope he's making it all right. Quine was certain that all this is true, and he said that "Intelligence" would not have let the news out if it weren't. So now you can rest awhile, mom, and just hope that we crack Germany pretty soon and get Al out of there.

Yet, despite these occasional reasons for hope, according to a report printed in the *Independent-Leader* on November 2, 1944, on November 1, 1944, Albee's parents received word from the War Department that their

Left: Prior to extensive renovations, the Main Street post office used from the 1920s through the 1940s was possibly at 54 Main Street in the lot next door to that of the current post office. *Public domain.*

Right: Dedicated on May 14, 1944, to honor those lost in World War II, the Woodbridge Proper Honor Roll still faces the firemen's memorial on Park Drive. *Michael Provance.*

boy was "now declared officially dead." The same article subsequently mentions that despite this notification, Albee's parents weren't yet willing to accept his death; they even planned to ask their bishop to write to Pope Pius XII to see if the pontiff could inquire about Albee.

After this, the trail goes cold, as they say: while a headstone for Albee sits at St. James Cemetery in Woodbridge and the *Fords Beacon* ran an obituary for Albee on November 12, stories about his possible survival persisted for another year before they abruptly vanished from the local press. Consequently, Albee's fate remains a mystery to this day, and the Department of Defense still lists him among the 2,135 World War II servicemen from New Jersey who are missing in action.

And so, Mrs. Leffler joined the ranks of Woodbridge's many Gold Star mothers grieving their lost sons. In honor of these women's sacrifices, the town installed its Honor Roll plaque on Mother's Day 1944 on School Street in Woodbridge Park. As Troeger and McEwen note, Mrs. Harry Stankiewicz, mother of the first Woodbridge serviceman lost in the war, U.S. Marine Robert J. Madden, dedicated the monument. Soon thereafter, word reached Woodbridge that Germany was finally breaking when local Army infantryman James "Dubbs" Gerity penned the following letter to his brother David; originally published in the *Independent-Leader* and reprinted by Troeger and McEwen, it describes Dubbs's experiences on D-Day, as the Allies wrested control of Normandy from Germany at the cost of over 53,714 Allied lives:

> *After leaving England, we were taken down and loaded on an LCI* [Landing Craft Infantry] *and spent four days on waiting for the bell to ring for the first round in the main event....We moved around a bit but stayed close to shore until the morning of D-Day, when we moved across and waited off the other shore until our time to land....Then,* [at] *about 6 p.m., it was our turn and we headed in. After the LCI went in as far as it could, we got off that and into a small craft which we thought would take us right in. Much to our dismay, it stopped a couple of hundred yards from shore and let down its front for us to disembark...into water almost neck-deep....And, while we were making our way in, old Herman the German dropped a couple of his now well-known 88s along the beach, which didn't exactly serve to cheer any of us up....We were also bothered quite a bit by snipers who had stayed behind to raise some mischief of their own. And, of course, their artillery—usually those 88s—also had to be contended with.*

An eyesore since John Witte opened it across the Arthur Kill in the 1930s, Staten Island's "ship graveyard" is home to several D-Day vessels. *National Archives.*

Less than a year later, the May 7, 1945, issue of the *Independent-Leader* ran the headline: "GERMANY FOLDS UP." Area residents refused to celebrate, however, reminding themselves that the war was still on in Japan. Each day, the newsreels and papers told stories of progress in the Pacific, but the enemy who had first sucker-punched the United States at Pearl Harbor was proving tougher to crack than anyone expected. Over a million additional servicemen were expected to lose their lives in the invasion of Japan, and President Harry S. Truman seemed worried—he even said he never wanted the job of president. Then came footage of two mushroom-shaped, fiery columns rising from the Japanese cities of Nagasaki and Hiroshima like devilish steam—these came from the, what-do-you-call-it, atomic bomb. On August 14, 1945, as a solitary lawnmower possibly growled somewhere in the distance, Woodbridge residents, coffee cups in hand, reached for the morning paper on yet another sweltering summer morning on the home front when, dead-center, top-of-the-fold, they saw that the *Independent-Leader* had run two simple words: "WAR ENDS."

The town erupted.

From Fords to Colonia, pews overflowed. Cars raced up and down Main Street honking their horns until 3:00 a.m. as tricolor bunting and American

Even though World War II didn't end up being the "war to end all wars," Woodbridge's ecstatic homecoming parade, boasting 30,000 attendees, might have been the end-all of parades. *Richard.*

flags streamed from their antennas and mirrors. All along St. Georges Avenue, Amboy Avenue, Rahway Avenue, Port Reading Avenue—and in every home throughout the township, mothers and fathers cried tears of relief while young enlistments not yet packed off to camp dumped their suitcases on the floor and raced into the streets to dance with the first gals they met. In fact, things got so understandably out of hand that police chief George E. Keating, concerned the celebration might become a riot, closed the town's liquor stores at 9:00 p.m., directing them to not reopen until the next day.

Meanwhile, Mayor Greiner appointed Charles Gregory to plan Woodbridge's very own ticker-tape parade. On the day of October 29, 1946, with the last of the town's sons safely home, more than four thousand marchers flowed from Legion Stadium to Fulton Street, to the Veterans' Memorial in Woodbridge Park behind guest of honor General George K. Nold, while thousands more flooded the sidewalks to watch. All told, over thirty thousand servicemen and civilians attended the event, which featured a marching-band competition judged from a stand on Main Street, a brief and solemn ceremony at Woodbridge Park and a reception for the town's Gold Star families at the Colonia home of Mrs. Edward K. Cone. World War II had been the "war to end all wars," and with its end, residents turned their attention to building the town we know today.

The End of History:
Woodbridge in the Postwar Era

If the world of American poet T.S. Eliot's "The Waste Land" ends with a "whimper," Woodbridge's postwar world started with a crash—and a bad one, at that: during rush hour on Tuesday, February 6, 1951, Pennsylvania Railroad train No. 733 (known as "The Broker") derailed as it neared Woodbridge's Main Street rail bridge, sending several cars smashing into a row of homes along Fulton Street. Eighty-four passengers and bystanders were killed, and hundreds more were injured in the wreck, making it one of the deadliest train crashes in U.S. history.

A little later, in December 1951, Captain Henrik Kurt Carlsen, a Danish immigrant who lived in Woodbridge, became a national sensation after his freighter, the *Flying Enterprise*, was so badly lashed by a North Atlantic storm that, when an enormous wave broadsided it 320 miles off the English coast, the ship's hull split straight across the deck midships; in response, Carlsen issued an SOS that brought rescue crews, and on December 31, 1951, his forty crewmen and ten passengers were spirited to safety. Yet, the stalwart captain clung on, remaining on his foundering vessel for the next five days as tugboats pulled it toward Falmouth harbor. It was during this time that Carlsen showed his true mettle; when the *Enterprise* was just forty-one miles from shore, one rescuer leaped onto the ship in an attempt to rescue the captain only to find himself quite literally in the same boat when another violent storm snapped the tugboats' towline and sent the *Enterprise* listing. By January 10, 1952, the ship was almost flat on its side and dropping swiftly into the Atlantic when the captain and his would-be rescuer jumped overboard in a gamble to save themselves. Subsequently, within the next forty minutes, Carlsen and the rescue crewman were taken up by another vessel while the *Enterprise* dropped to the ocean's depths, precipitating commendations for Carlsen's daring escape from both President Truman and King Frederick IX of Denmark as well as a full-fledged ticker tape parade in New York City on January 17 and a parade in Woodbridge at which then-Mayor Hugh Quigley stated, "We are proud that you, a man of courage, a man unafraid, selected Woodbridge for your home."

These are just two of the noteworthy incidents that have occurred in Woodbridge since the end of World War II. Indeed, there are many others worth mentioning, including the completion of the town's linkup with the federal highway system—which began in 1928 with the construction of the Woodbridge Cloverleaf (one of the nation's first safety-engineered

This page: These are period and contemporary photos of the site where The Broker's devastating crash occurred. As the 1951 photo shows, Fulton Street was demolished! *Woodbridge Township Historic Commission.*

Opposite, top: This photo of the *Flying Enterprise*'s foundering on January 10, 1952, shows just how risky Captain Carlsen's leap to safety really was. *Department of the Navy.*

Opposite, bottom: Before the New Jersey Highway Authority took over the Parkway, taxpayer money completed the eleven-mile stretch around Woodbridge—which is why that section is still toll-free today. *Public Library of Massachusetts.*

Garden State Parkway Interchange near
Woodbridge, New Jersey Turnpike

superhighway intersections) and was completed after World War II, when much of Keasbey became the site of the Highway 287–Route 440 interchange—and the construction of Woodbridge Center Mall, the Prudential Plaza Office Complex, the Woodbridge Public Library, the Woodbridge Metropark, the Hess Building and a host of other local landmarks.

The problem with discussing this period, though, is that the scope of history is so long that the closer the historian's gaze, the more out of focus it becomes. For one thing, those in power frequently hide facts to protect themselves, while the disempowered are, often enough, harmed or insulted if a historian catches them in the proverbial act. Perhaps more importantly, it can take decades, even centuries, for a historical thread to play itself out—as we saw with Woodbridge's involvement in the New Jersey Land Wars. What, for instance, is the historical importance of the New Jersey Shakespeare Festival's launching its first production in Woodbridge in 1961? As someone who loves Shakespeare, I'm more than happy to admit that maybe there isn't one. But, even if there is, it's certainly not going to be apparent after only fifty-eight years.

And so it is that the true turning points in any community's history seem fuzzy without a few centuries' remove. But, worse, many local historians consequently resort to ending their town histories with laundry lists of disconnected, incidental ribbon-cutting ceremonies to name as many prominent figures as possible. Well, Woodbridge, I have decided we are far too intimate, at this point, for that. Besides, this is supposed to be a *brief* history—a history in celebration of your township charter. So, instead of filling out this book's last few pages with a dull who's-who, I have instead decided to end on a few of the most poignant points, a few of the moments the town can be proudest of, and then mention the few recent incidents I think will be worth remembering in another hundred years.

For instance, Woodbridge can certainly be proud that it was one of ten towns to receive an "All-America City" award from the National Civic League in 1964. And it can also be proud of local Medal of Honor recipient First Lieutenant Jack H. Jacobs, who received the nation's highest award for his service in the Vietnam War (1955–75). Jacobs, while part of a Military Assistance Command force in the Republic of Vietnam's Kien Phong province, singlehandedly saved an entire Allied South Vietnamese company of the Second Battalion, 16th Infantry, from being overwhelmed by a battalion of Viet Cong: according to the *New York Times*, although he was already wounded in the head and arms by mortar fragments,

This photograph of an Avenel resident posing beside his car around Thanksgiving 1958 bears witness to the domestic calm that settles over Woodbridge between wars. *Richard.*

Jacobs took command of the South Vietnamese company, rallied its men, and again and again personally scrabbled across blood-filled rice paddies, as dozens of enemy bullets whistled past, to recover a fellow American advisor, the company's commander and twelve other wounded South Vietnamese soldiers while also killing three Viet Cong himself. Awarded the nation's highest honor by President Richard Nixon—joining Woodbridge's Carle E. Petersen, honored posthumously for his service in the Boxer Rebellion—Jacobs has since worked in finance and authored several books.

Moreover, the town can be understandably proud of the other servicemen who fought in Vietnam, especially those who lost their lives, including Private First Class Louis Allen Ambrose, Corporal Alan Bedrock, Sergeant Ralph Custode, Private First Class John William Allen Dorio, Corporal George Steven Edley, Private First Class Peter Alan Gruca, Lance Corporal Paul Wayne Handerhan, Lance Corporal Robert Hanson, Private First Class Daniel Alan Hilderbrandt, Lance Corporal Peter Mazillo Jr., Second Lieutenant Victor George Mika, Sergeant Vincent Moran, Private First Class Timothy John Murphy, Private First Class Maurice Joseph O'Callaghan,

Private First Class Vincent F. Risoldi and Private First Class Anthony Skodmin, as well as the town's veterans and honored dead from the Korean War (1950–53), Private First Class John Okane and those who fought or have fought in operation Desert Storm and in the nation's longest war to date, the "War on Terror" (2001–present), which still drags on at the time of this writing.

This brings us to the incident that led to the wars in Afghanistan and Iraq—the attacks on September 11, 2001, since known as "9/11." During the attacks, members of the terrorist organization Al-Qaeda hijacked four passenger planes and crashed three of them into Manhattan's World Trade Center buildings (or the "Twin Towers") and the Pentagon building in Arlington, Virginia, while the fourth plane, Flight 93, crashed near Shankstown, Pennsylvania. Woodbridge's place in these devastating events, which killed 2,996 people, injured thousands of others, and caused a minimum of $10 billion in property damage, is its nine residents lost in the attacks, including Edward Allegretto, Marilyn Bautista, Patrick Dunn, John Adam Larson, James Lynch, Charles Mauro, Tonyell McDay, Narender Nath and Sankara Velamuri. The town has since honored these friends and neighbors with a monument near the municipal building.

Further, many other Woodbridge residents actually saw the crashing jetliners send flames across the Manhattan skyline and, later, watched a column of dust rise from the collapsing buildings from vantages in other Manhattan buildings as well as from various locations in Woodbridge itself. Not only do many Woodbridge residents still work in New York City today, but the towers were less than eight miles from Woodbridge proper. So, those working on the top floors of the township's taller structures, like the New Jersey Turnpike offices on Route 9 (still the Hess Building at the time), had a clear view of the devastation from across the Hudson.

To this day, many residents continue to suffer from memories of the attacks and from the loss of loved ones, while many others have had health issues from breathing the various particulates the towers' destruction unleashed on the region. Moreover, the events of 9/11 also had another major impact on Woodbridge history, for it was in their wake that states began appointing Homeland Security advisors to help prevent future attacks on their soil. As former Woodbridge mayor James E. McGreevey assumed New Jersey's governorship in 2002, it quickly came to light that his Homeland Security advisor, Golan Cipel, wasn't qualified for the position and couldn't even gain a federal security clearance.

This page: Combatting industrial blight: In the 1970s, Sewaren insisted on a fifty-foot park to buffer it from Shell Oil, while "Project Bowtie" gave Port Reading a facelift. *EPA*.

This put not only New Jersey but Woodbridge, where McGreevey had been mayor from 1991 to 2002, in the public spotlight. The town's embarrassment over the issue only grew when McGreevey revealed the actual reason for the appointment: the governor had been carrying on an adulterous homosexual relationship with Cipel. Of course, at the time of the present writing, attitudes toward homosexuality have dramatically changed. But fifteen years ago, the town reeled from the news of McGreevey's affair with Cipel, leading residents to criticize the governor, whom many locals had known personally.

At first, this criticism focused on McGreevey's infidelity to his wife Dina Matos McGreevey, who was also well known, and his irresponsibility as a governor in appointing an unqualified lover to a major post. But, when it was revealed during McGreevey's 2008 divorce from Dina that not only had she been aware of his sexual orientation but had participated in threesomes with him and other men, the town exploded with homophobic hate speech toward the then-former governor. To be fair, Woodbridge's residents were mostly giving vent to their embarrassment over a situation that scandalized their town nationally, and their concern was less with McGreevey and his wife's lifestyle than that so many across the United States, in far less progressive areas, were speaking ill of the town. But, still, the net effect is the same—these attitudes should be seen as a shameful blemish on the town's history, even as residents can be proud that one of their former mayors became New Jersey's first openly gay governor.

So, Woodbridge has continued to make its mark on New Jersey and the entire country, and it will presumably continue to do so for the next 350 years. For, even after the devastation of the Great Recession, which

One of the newest architectural marvels in the greater Woodbridge area is the Raritan Hotel, which stands across from Raritan Center on the edge of Edison and Keasbey. *Brewbooks.*

started in 2007 and caused New Jersey's unemployment rate to spike to roughly 10 percent, and even after 2012's Hurricane Sandy, which left thirty Woodbridge homes condemned within a five-block radius, the town is still one of the sweetest little pockets of small-town living in the entire country.

As noted in this volume's introduction, then, as I sit through yet another of Chicagoland's three-degree blizzards, typing the last few sentences of my own offering to Woodbridge on its "Semiseptcentennial"—yeah, say that ten times fast—I can't help remembering the decade I spent there, wishing I were again sitting over a brimming cup of coffee and a plate of eggs and hash at the Reo Diner with a balmy thirty-nine-degree low awaiting me outside. Because it's just impossible not to hanker for another stroll around "the Wood," and because knowing the town's history, the stories behind its neighborhoods and landmarks, its architecturally stunning homes and public buildings, its stories both heroic and heartrending, just does it for me. In my own mind's eye, I am again turning the corner at the Soldiers and Sailors Monument, heading up Main Street and envisioning the massive Salamander Works factory that once sprawled to my right and the ghosts of Cornwallis's battalions marching by the thousands behind me. Woodbridge, in short, haunts me—as I hope, now that you've read my little book, it will haunt you.

BIBLIOGRAPHY

Although this work is a popular history, it is a history nonetheless, and therefore, I relied on extensive research to fill out my understanding of Woodbridge's past and its wider contexts; I do not in any way claim to be a historian, but in serving as one here, my primary purpose has been to tell the 350-year history of Woodbridge, New Jersey, in a way that is interesting for the average reader. Consequently, though I have striven in all cases to cite in the text of *A Brief History of Woodbridge, New Jersey*, every source from which I have gleaned my information and historical opinions, it is impossible to say that some opinion or fact expressed as my own was not in some way informed by one of the following sources preliminarily read or cited in a deleted portion of an earlier draft whose facts and/or opinions are related in the finished book uncited. Indeed, I openly admit that in many cases I cut incessant, academic citation because it might have undermined readability.

Thus, in providing the following bibliography of my complete research, I am presenting the full list of those authors and documents on which I relied for my work, openly stating that all information and historical opinions have been gleaned from the following—hence it is a bibliography; again, I am a creative writer, so the only portions of this work I lay claim to as not deriving from another author in some way are the present volume's imaginative moments, diction, syntax and rhetoric, as well as my knack for organizing information presented elsewhere in a scattered way into coherent narratives.

Armstrong, April C., and Kristine Marconi McGee. "Can Nathaniel Fitz Randolph's Descendants Attend Princeton University for Free?" Mudd Manuscript Library Blog, Princeton University Archives and Public Papers. June 10, 2015. https://blogs.princeton.edu/mudd/2015/06/can-nathaniel-fitzrandolphs-descendants-attend-princeton-university-for-free/.

Armstrong, William C. *Pioneer Families of Northwestern New Jersey.* Baltimore, MD: Genealogical Publishing Co., Inc., 1998.

Baldwin, Carly. "Woodbridge 9/11 Memorial Service Announced: Nine Woodbridge Residents Lost Their Lives on 9/11." Woodbridge Patch, Patch.com. Last modified August 31, 2016. https://patch.com/new-jersey/woodbridge/woodbridge-9-11-memorial-service-announced.

Bartlett, John R. *Dictionary of Americanisms: A Glossary of Words and Phrases Usually Regarded as Peculiar to the United States,* 3rd ed. Boston: Little, Brown & Co., 1860.

Bell, Deborah. "Buy a Ton of Woodbridge History—Bank Vault Door Is for Sale on eBay." Woodbridge Patch, Patch.com. Last modified May 7, 2013. https://patch.com/new-jersey/woodbridge/buy-a-ton-of-woodbridge-history-bank-vault-door-is-fo12a35dd526.

Bell, J.L. "The Mysterious Constitutional Courant." Boston: 1775 (blog). Last modified January 2, 2016. http://boston1775.blogspot.com/2016/01/the-mysterious-constitutional-courant.html.

Bond, Gordon. *Wicked Woodbridge & Crazy Carteret.* Staunton, VA: American History Press, 2015.

"Building an Army: The Structure of a 19th Century Army." The National Park Service. Accessed February 7, 2018. https://www.nps.gov/fosu/learn/education/upload/Building-an-Army-Civil-War-Background.pdf.

Burrows, Edwin G., and Mike Wallace. *Gotham: A History of New York City to 1898.* New York: Oxford University Press, 1999.

Carr, J. Revell. *Seeds of Discontent: The Deep Roots of the American Revolution, 1650–1750.* New York: Walked Publishing Company, Inc., 2008.

"The Cemetery of the First Presbyterian Church." The First Presbyterian Church of Woodbridge, NJ, FPCWoodbridgeNJ.org. Accessed on February 6, 2018. http://www.fpcwoodbridgenj.org/cemetery.php.

"Closing of Bank Hits Directors Hard." *Woodbridge Independent* (Woodbridge, NJ), December 18, 1931.

Dally, Joseph W. *Woodbridge and Vicinity: The Story of a New Jersey Township.* New Brunswick, NJ: A.E. Gordon, 1873.

"D-Day and the Battle of Normandy: Your Questions Answered." D-Day Museum & Overlord Embroidery, Portsmouth D-Day Museum. Accessed

February 7, 2018. http://www.ddaymuseum.co.uk/d-day/d-day-and-the-battle-of-normandy-your-questions-answered.

Di Ionno, Mark. "Hurricane Sandy the Second Big Hit for Woodbridge Neighborhood." NJ.com (blog), *Star-Ledger*. Last modified February 23, 2013. http://blog.nj.com/njv_mark_diionno/2013/02/hurricane_sandy_the_second_big.html.

Documents Relating to the Colonial History of the State of New Jersey, vol. 3, edited by William A. Whitehead. Newark, NJ: Daily Advertiser Printing House, 1881.

"Eight More Die in Battle; Total Is 69." *Independent-Leader* (Woodbridge, NJ), November 2, 1944.

Encyclopedia of New Jersey. Edited by Maxine N. Lurie and Marc Mappen. New Brunswick, NJ: Rutgers University Press, 2004.

Fleisher, Lisa. "N.J. Unemployment Jumps to 9.7 Percent, Matches U.S. Rate." NJ.com (blog), *The Star-Ledger*. Last modified September 16, 2009. http://www.nj.com/business/index.ssf/2009/09/nj_unemployment_matches_us_rat.html.

"Founding of Elizabeth." City of Elizabeth. Accessed February 6, 2018. http://www.elizabethnj.org/about/founding-elizabeth.

Franklin, Benjamin. (From Benjamin Franklin to Deborah Franklin, 20 April 1770). Founders Online, National Archives, American Philosophical Society and Yale University. Last modified January 17, 2002. http://founders.archives.gov/documents/Franklin/01-17-02-0062.

Frazza, Al. "Revolutionary War Sites in Scotch Plains, New Jersey." Revolutionary War New Jersey (blog). Accessed February 6, 2018. http://www.revolutionarywarnewjersey.com/new_jersey_revolutionary_war_sites/towns/scotch_plains_nj_revolutionary_war_sites.htm.

Gilman, C. Malcom B. *The Story of the Jersey Blues*. Red Bank, NJ: Arlington Laboratory for Clinical and Historical Research, 1962.

Ginn, Richard V.N. *The History of the U.S. Army Medical Service Corps*. Washington, DC: Office of the Surgeon General and Center of Military History, 2008.

Graham, Patricia A. *Studies in the History of American Education Series Critical Episodes in American Politics*, vol. 6, *Community and Class in American Education, 1865–1918*. Toronto, ON: John Wiley & Sons Canada, Limited, 1974.

"Graves of US 'Flu' Victims in Devon, England," photo (Western Newspaper Union, 1919), reprinted in the *Woodbridge Independent* (Woodbridge, NJ), March 28, 1919.

Groeling, Meg. *The Aftermath of Battle: The Burial of the Civil War Dead*. El Dorado Hills, CA: Savas Beatie, 2015.

Handbook of American Indians North of Mexico, vol. 3, Edited by Frederick Hodge. Scituate, MA: Digital Scanning Inc., 2003.

Handbook of North American Indians: Northeast, vol. 15 of *Handbook of North American Indians*, Edited by Bruce G. Trigger and William C. Washington, DC: Smithsonian Institution Scholarly Press, 1978.

Hatala, Greg. "Glimpse of History: Diner Is a Woodbridge Landmark." NJ.com (blog), *Star-Ledger*. Last modified April 17, 2015. http://www.nj.com/news/local/index.ssf/2012/08/diner_is_a_woodbridge_landmark.html.

———. "Glimpse of History: Side-by-Side Racing in Front of the Grandstand in Woodbridge." NJ.com (blog), *Star-Ledger*. Last modified February 24, 2014. http://www.nj.com/middlesex/index.ssf/2014/02/glimpse_of_history_side-by-side_racing_in_front_of_the_grandstand_in_woodbridge.html.

"Hess-West Avenue and Milos Way, Port Reading Redevelopment Plan." Woodbridge, NJ: Township of Woodbridge Department of Planning & Development, 2014.

"Historic Walking Tour of Woodbridge," vol. 1. Woodbridge Township Preservation Commission, 2009. Accessed February 6, 2018. https://www.twp.woodbridge.nj.us/DocumentCenter/View/935.

"Historic Walking Tour of Woodbridge," vol. 2. Woodbridge Township Preservation Commission, 2010. Accessed February 7, 2018. https://www.twp.woodbridge.nj.us/DocumentCenter/View/935.

"Historic Walking Tour of Woodbridge," vol. 6. Woodbridge Township Preservation Commission, 2016. Accessed February 7, 2018. http://nebula.wsimg.com/0f79acc00f70c8a1130b1ac0c9f1ca6c?AccessKeyId=8CF9B090AAC64086AC33&disposition=0&alloworigin=1.

"Historic Walking Tour of Woodbridge," vol. 8. Woodbridge Township Preservation Commission, 2016. Accessed February 11, 2018. http://nebula.wsimg.com/0f79acc00f70c8a1130b1ac0c9f1ca6c?AccessKeyId=8CF9B090AAC64086AC33&disposition=0&alloworigin=1.

Holzman, Elias. "Bombs Proliferate Area's Terra Cotta Collection." (*Home News Tribune*, January 17, 2002), quoted in Virginia Bergen Troeger and Robert J. McEwen. *Woodbridge: New Jersey's Oldest Township*. (Charleston, SC: Arcadia Publishing, 2002).

"Hope Renewed for Leffler." *Independent-Leader* (Woodbridge, NJ), May 12, 1944.

Howe, Julia Ward. "The Battle Hymn of the Republic." *The Atlantic*, February 1862. https://www.theatlantic.com/magazine/archive/1862/02/the-battle-hymn-of-the-republic/308052/.

Howell, Todd. "A Brief History of Woodbridge Fire Department." Woodbridge Fire Dept. Accessed February 12, 2018. http://www.woodbridgefd.org/content/history/.

"How Much Did the September 11 Terrorist Attack Cost America?" Institute for the Analysis of Global Security (blog), IAGS.org. Accessed February 7, 2018. http://www.iags.org/costof911.html.

Impact of 9/11 on Politics and War: The Day that Changed Everything, The, Edited by Matthew J. Morgan. New York: Palgrave Macmillan, 2009.

James, George. "Communities; Those Whom We Honor." *New York Times,* May 28, 2000. Accessed February 7, 2018. http://www.nytimes.com/2000/05/28/nyregion/communities-those-whom-we-honor.html.

Janney, Samuel. *The Life of William Penn,* 6th ed. Philadelphia: Friends' Book Association, 1882.

"Joe Hooker at the Poker Table." *Washington Star,* reprinted in *The Independent Hour* (Woodbridge, NJ), October 26, 1876.

Kurlansky, Mark. *The Big Oyster: History on the Half Shell.* New York: Random House, 2006.

Landsman, Ned C. *Scotland and Its First American Colony, 1683–1765.* Princeton, NJ: Princeton University Press, 1985.

LaPenta, Frank. "Resident Recalls Deadly Woodbridge Train Wreck of 1951." *Home News Tribune,* MyCentralJersey.com (Somerville, NJ). Last modified February 9, 2017. https://www.mycentraljersey.com/story/news/local/middlesex-county/2016/02/05/resident-recalls-deadly-woodbridge-train-wreck-1951/79640990/.

Leech, Douglas E. *Roots of Conflict: British Armed Forces and Colonial Americans, 1677–1763.* Chapel Hill: University of North Carolina Press, 1986.

"Lenape Tribe." Site Seen Ltd., *War Paths to Peace Pipes.* Last modified January 16, 2016. https://www.warpaths2peacepipes.com/indian-tribes/lenapi-tribe.htm.

MacIntosh, Jeane. "I Was McG and Wife's Three-Way Sex Stud: Ex-Driver." *New York Post,* NYPost.com. Last modified March 17, 2008. https://nypost.com/2008/03/17/i-was-mcg-and-wifes-three-way-sex-stud-ex-driver/.

"Man of Letters." Twin Cities Public Television, Inc., PBS.org. Accessed February 6, 2018. http://www.pbs.org/benfranklin/l3_world_letters.html.

Mayers, Robert A. "The Battle of the Short Hills: The American Revolution Almost Ended in New Jersey." *GardenStateLegacy.com,* no. 13, September 2011. http://gardenstatelegacy.com/files/The_Battle_of_the_Short_Hills_Mayers_GSL13.pdf.

McElroy, Leon. *History of Woodbridge Township.* Woodbridge, NJ: Woodbridge High School, 1955.

McGreevey, James E. "The Making of a Gay American." *New York Magazine*, NYMag.com. Accessed February 7, 2018. http://nymag.com/news/politics/21340/.

Meuly, Walter C. *History of Piscataway Township, 1666–1976.* Piscataway, NJ: Piscataway Bicentennial Commission, 1976.

Meyers, Keith. "A Lesson in History of Old Ships." NYTimes.com, *New York Times.* Accessed February 11, 2018. http://www.nytimes.com/1990/12/31/nyregion/a-lesson-in-history-of-old-ships.html.

Moran, Mark. "Light Dispelling Darkness." WeirdNJ.com, *Weird New Jersey.* Accessed February 12, 2018. http://weirdnj.com/stories/light-dispelling-darkness/.

Neely, Mark E., and Harold Holzer. *The Union Image: Popular Prints of the Civil War North.* Chapel Hill: University of North Carolina Press, 2000.

"New Jersey Korean War Casualties." VetFriends.com. Accessed February 7, 2018. https://www.vetfriends.com/memorial/mem_alphab.cfm?war_id=3&states_ID=32&page_id=551&city=city.

9/11 Commission Report: Final Report of the National Commission on Terrorist Attacks Upon the United States, The, Compiled by Thomas Kean. Washington, D.C.: Government Printing Office, 2011.

Official Book: 255 Anniversary and Memorial Celebration. Woodbridge, NJ: 255th Anniversary and Memorial Celebration Programme Committee, 1924.

O'Rourke, Michelle. "In Memory of The Soldiers and Sailors of Woodbridge, NJ who fought in The Wars of Our Country." *The Corner.* http://cornerpapernj.com/news/history/memory-soldiers-sailors-woodbridge-nj-fought-wars-country.

Orr, Brian J. "Passengers on the *Henry & Francis* 1685." TheReformation.info. Accessed February 6, 2018. http://www.thereformation.info/passhf.htm.

"Our Tribal History." *The Nanticoke Lenni-Lenape: An American Indian Tribe.* Last modified 2007. http://www.nanticoke-lenape.info/history.htm.

"Persons from New Jersey who Died in the Vietnam War." The Virtual Wall, Vietnam Veterans Memorial, VirtualWall.org. Last modified December 30, 2017. http://www.virtualwall.org/istate/istatnj.htm.

Pfister, Jude M. *The Jacob Ford Jr. Mansion: The Storied History of a New Jersey Home.* Charleston, SC: The History Press, 2009.

Potter, L.E. "Nurse Discovers 15 Cases of Chicken Pox." *Woodbridge Independent* (Woodbridge, NJ), March 21, 1919.

Punturieri, Carol. "A Revolutionary War Re-Enactment to Be Staged at Camp Jefferson" Township of Jefferson Bicentennial Committee,

JeffersonBicentennial.org. Last modified November 1, 2004. http://www.jeffersonbicentennial.org/news/releases/04_1101.html.

Rosmos, Julie Fisco, and Barbara Rosmos Estok. *Oral History Interview*. By Brenda Velasco. March 18, 2010. Woodbridge Public Library Archives. Accessed February 7, 2018. http://www.digifind-it.com/woodbridge/oral_histories/PDFs/TRNSCPT%20-%20Julie%20Ficso%20Rosmos%20and%20Barbara%20Rosmos%20Estok.pdf#search="spanish flu".

Ruppert, Bob. "The First Fight of Ferguson's Rifle." All Things Liberty (blog), *Journal of the American Revolution*. Accessed February 7, 2018. https://allthingsliberty.com/2014/11/fergusons-rifle-first-fight/.

"Service Personnel Not Recovered Following WWII from New Jersey." Defense POW/MIA Accounting Agency, Department of Defense. Last modified January 18, 2018. http://www.dpaa.mil/portals/85/Documents/WWIIAccounting/new_jersey.html.

"Sgt Albert Jacob 'Albee' Leffler." Find a Grave, FindAGrave.com. Accessed February 7, 2018. https://www.findagrave.com/memorial/95006012.

"Slavery in New Jersey." New Jersey Women's History, NJWomensHistory.org. Accessed February 6, 2018. http://www.njwomenshistory.org/wp-content/uploads/2013/07/Slavery-in-New-Jersey.pdf.

"State, ICC to Open Investigation Today into Cause of 83-Death Train Disaster; Engineer and Conductor Differ on Speed." *Fords Beacon* (Fords, NJ), February 8, 1951.

"St. Demetrius Ukrainian Orthodox Cathedral Celebrates 100 Years." The Ukrainian Orthodox Church of the United States of America, 2009. Accessed February 12, 2018. http://uocofusa.org/news_091116_2.html.

"Thanks of the Public Due the Drug Trade During the Influenza Epidemic." *Woodbridge Independent* (Woodbridge, NJ), March 21, 1919.

Troeger, Virginia Bergen, and Robert J. McEwen. *Woodbridge: New Jersey's Oldest Township*. Charleston, SC: Arcadia Publishing, 2002.

Utz, Axel. "Cultural Exchange, Imperialist Violence, and Pious Missions: Local Perspectives from Tanjavur and Lenape Country, 1720–1760." PhD diss., Pennsylvania State University, State College, 2011.

Vecsy, Elmer J. "History of the Woodbridge Township Stadium." *History of the Woodbridge Township Stadium and School System*. Woodbridge, NJ: Woodbridge Stadium Commission, 1936.

"'Very Proud of Brother', Wrote 'Albee' Leffler, Reported Missing in Last Letter to Sewaren Pal." *Fords Beacon* (Fords, NJ), November 19, 1943.

"Walking Purchase." *United States History.* Encyclopedia Britannica, Britannica.com. Accessed February 6, 2018. https://www.britannica.com/event/Walking-Purchase.

War Department Annual Report to the Secretary of War Fiscal Year Ending June 30, 1919, vols. 1–2. War Department. Washington, DC: US Government Printing Office, 1919.

Weeks, Daniel J. *Not for Filthy Lucre's Sake: Richard Saltar and the Antiproprietary Movement in East New Jersey, 1665–1707.* Cranbury, NJ: Associated University Presses, 2001.

Wilson, Doug. "The Elm Tree Tavern of Woodbridge, NJ, 1739–1823." Doug Wilson (blog). Accessed February 6, 2018. http://dougwilson.com/Family/feature/elmtreetavern.asp.

Wodrow, Robert. *A History of the Sufferings of the Church of Scotland,* vol. 4. Port St. Lucie, FL: Solid Ground Christian Books, 2008.

INDEX

ABOUT THE AUTHOR

Photo by Shelton Walsmith.

Having spent many formative years in Woodbridge, New Jersey, prize-winning author Phill Provance once worked as an archivist's assistant at the Woodbridge Public Library. A graduate of West Virginia Wesleyan College, with a duel-genre MFA in both poetry and fiction, he completed his undergraduate degree at Bethany College and Oxford University, and his work—which has appeared in publications as diverse as the *Baltimore Sun*, *InQuest Gamer* and the *Crab Creek Review*, among many others—has garnered numerous awards and honors from the likes of poet Bill Brown and Pulitzer Prize nominee Diane Seuss, who has called his work "*wit[ty]…creep[y]…snark[y]…[and] haunted.*"

Though life in recent years has taken him to Chicago, where he currently resides with his son, Ledger, he returns to Woodbridge every summer to visit family and friends in the area, and he's always happy to make new friends over a warm cup of joe at the Reo Diner or a cocktail at Mulberry Street Restaurant when he's in town. Meanwhile, he's over the proverbial moon that he's been able to bring to bear the writing chops he first honed among friends like Deborah LaVeglia and Joe Weil at the Barron Arts Center while helping the best little town in New Jersey commemorate its 350th anniversary.